Alabaster Village
Our Years in Transylvania

Christine Morgan

with Anne Morrison Welsh

Skinner House Books
Boston

Published by Skinner House Books, an imprint of the Unitarian Universalist Association,
25 Beacon Street, Boston, MA 02108-2800.

Printed in the USA.

10 9 8 7 6 5 4 3 2 1
99 98 97

Cover design by Charlotte Burgess
Text design by Suzanne Morgan

Acknowledgements

The lyrics to "Let It Be a Dance" are by Ric Masten. Copyright © 1977 Mastensville Music (BMI). Reprinted by permission of Ric Masten.

Photos on pages 8, 30, 46, 70, and 73 are from a private scrapbook of Feri and Christine Balázs' life in Transylvania during the 1920s and 1930s. Photos on pages 85, 102, and 131 are from the library of the Estate of Christine Morgan. The sketch of the Meszko Unitarian Templom on page 4 is from a postcard Feri Balázs sent to Dr. Earl Morse Wilbur, president of the Unitarian College in Berkeley, California, from 1911 to 1931.

Library of Congress Cataloging-in-Publication Data

Morgan, Christine, 1903-1996.
Alabaster village : our years in Transylvania / Christine Morgan : with Anne Welsh.
p. cm.
ISBN 1-55896-350-2 (alk. paper)
1. Morgan, Christine, 1903-1996. 2. Balázs, Francis. 3. Unitarians—Romania—Transylvania—Biography. 4. Spouses of clergy—Romania—Transylvania—Biography. 5. Unitarian churches—clergy—Romania—Transylvania—Biography. I. Welsh, Anne. II. Title
BX9869.M67A3 1997
289.1'092'24984—dc21
[B] 96-50125
CIP

Let It Be a Dance

Let it be a dance we do
May I have this dance with you?
Through the good times and the bad times, too
let it be a dance.

Let a dancing song be heard.
Play the music, say the words,
and fill the sky with sailing birds.
Let it be a dance. Let it be a dance. Let it be a dance.

Learn to follow, learn to lead,
feel the rhythm, fill the need
to reap the harvest, plant the seed.
Let it be a dance.

Everybody turn and spin,
let your body learn to bend,
and, like a willow with the wind,
Let it be a dance. Let it be a dance. Let it be a dance.

A child is born, the old must die;
a time for joy, a time to cry.
Take it as it passes by.
Let it be a dance.

Morning star comes out at night,
without the dark there can be no light.
If nothing's wrong, then nothing's right.
Let it be a dance. Let it be a dance. Let it be a dance.

Let the sun shine, let it rain;
share the laughter, bear the pain,
and round and round we go again.
Let it be a dance.

—Ric Masten

In Appreciation

I owe warm thanks to Lucy Morgan, who died years ago, for collecting and preserving my letters from abroad, which are woven into this story. Furthermore, without the financial help of Lucy and Arthur Morgan and my Aunt Isabel, Francis Balázs and I could not have survived in Transylvania as long as we did.

Equally warm thanks go to Anne Morrison Welsh for her skill in editing my old correspondence into a coherent narrative of my life. Her effort was largely a labor of love. The hundreds of hours she devoted to the task were many times more than the hours for which she was compensated.

Likewise, I am deeply indebted to the cheerful and tireless work of my husband, Ernest Morgan, on this publication. His dedicated efforts made it possible. Sally and John Burrowes significantly contributed by critically reading the manuscript as it progressed. With competence and meticulous care, Clare Hanrahan transcribed the old, fragile, handwritten letters into print.

The appalling social and economic situation in Transylvania that I and my first husband faced over sixty years ago is much the same today. I am moved and gratified that a new American/Hungarian couple has taken up the challenge of the Transylvanian villages. Don and Aniko Harrington—as idealistic as Francis and I, but older and wiser—are working with a group of remote villages there. Aniko has the role of Unitarian minister, with Don tackling the social and economic problems. Unencumbered by the reactionary church hierarchy that so hampered our efforts, and with modest help from abroad, these pioneers are bravely attempting to give history a new turn in eastern Europe.

—Christine Morgan

Contents

Introduction

At the Versailles Peace Conference that ended World War I, Transylvania, which had been part of Hungary for a thousand years, was ceded to Romania. US President Woodrow Wilson had put forward a plan for a just peace, which included self-determination of peoples, international cooperation, and democracy. But at Versailles, the British and French went ahead with the politics of imperialism, thus paving the way for Hitler and World War II. On June 4, 1920, the Treaty of Trianon was signed and Romania took over Transylvania, clamping down on Hungarian language and culture and imposing a corrupt administration.

With this history setting the stage, Christine Frederiksen, an idealistic American-Danish girl, and Francis (Feri) Balázs, an equally idealistic young Hungarian Unitarian minister, spent six years in Feri's native Transylvania trying to educate and uplift his fellow Hungarians.

I first met Christine in 1922 during her second year at Antioch College in Yellow Springs, Ohio, where my father, Arthur Morgan, had just become college president. At the time, she was active in the student body and editor of the village newspaper, *Yellow Springs News*.

After two years at Antioch, Christine's family ran out of money so she went to live with an aunt and uncle in Berkeley, California, and to attend the university there. She graduated in 1926 with a bachelor's degree in social science. That was the year she met Feri, a young theology student who was working on his ThD degree at the Unitarian College in Berkeley. They fell in love, and in 1929 Christine decided to join him in Transylvania.

From 1930 to 1936, Christine and Feri Balázs battled poverty, ethnic mistrust, and oppression in Meszko, a small, mixed Romanian-Hungarian village two hours away from Kolozsvár (now the city of Cluj-Napoca), Romania. The couple's situation was further complicated by the conservatism of Unitarian church leaders in Transylvania, who regarded Feri as a radical, young upstart. Furthermore, Feri's modest salary often failed to materialize. Christine and Feri struggled bravely, even tragically, with meager resources to build social morale, organize cooperatives, and upgrade education. After six years of effort in this Transylvanian village, Feri died from tuberculosis and Christine struggled to survive with her young daughter Enika and return to America.

Over the years, Christine kept in touch with my father and stepmother, Arthur and Lucy Morgan, who had visited her and Feri in Transylvania. With their help, she and Enika made their way back to America in 1937 and settled in Winter Park, Florida, where Christine worked as Acting Dean of Women for Rollins College.

After eight years of poverty in Transylvania, Christine was appalled to find a similar but different misery in the United States, namely in the black community. In Winter Park, she saw many black families living in hovels on muddy lanes with no street lighting. In black schools throughout the county, she discovered decrepit buildings and old textbooks cast off from white public schools. Black teachers were not allowed in local public libraries, so their resources for teaching were limited. With the same zeal that led her to Transylvania, Christine borrowed public library books in her name and read them aloud in black schools. She raised money for these schools to build their own libraries. Because she devoted so much time to the needs and problems of the black community, the administration of Rollins College decided not to confirm her as a full-time dean.

In 1939, Christine married Louis Wise, a distinguished scientist who had settled in Winter Park after an early retirement. Christine, Enika, and Louis moved to Appleton, Wisconsin, where Christine gave birth to another daughter, Cathy Wise. Racial prejudice in Appleton was no different from Winter Park. Black people were not even allowed in the city. In response to this situation, Christine organized a Human Relations Council that brought occasional speakers to town and published numerous articles in the local paper about racial inclusion. The city's policy of racial exclusion was finally abandoned.

During her time in Appleton, Christine founded the Unitarian Fellowship of Appleton and took active part in the League of Women Voters and in the local Democratic Party. She also earned a master's degree in human relations.

In 1981, Louis Wise died at age ninety. I did not meet up with Christine again until that year when she moved back to Yellow Springs, Ohio, after Louis's death. Like her, I had been widowed some years before. We were in our late seventies when we married in 1982, and it was a relationship of great warmth and affection, and one where ideals and values were actively shared. I admired her activist spirit that led her to march alone in the streets of Moscow, carrying a sign that read "One World, One Humanity with Trust, Not Fear."

I realized that, at our age, marriage would last only a few years, but this awareness made our marriage all the more precious. I was haunted by the concern that I might die before she did, thus abandoning her. Now that fear is gone. Christine died on May 3, 1996. Our thirteen years together have added much joy and meaning to my life.

During her eight years in Transylvania, Christine had written graphic letters home, telling how she and Feri carried on their struggle. Those letters came into the hands of my stepmother, who, struck by their dramatic quality and historic relevance, proposed to have them published in 1933. She was warned, however, that such publication might draw harsh reprisals from the Romanian government. Now, more than half a century later, that constraint no longer holds. With Christine's story now in print, I share the spirit and quality that made her life an adventurous and eventful one.

—Ernest Morgan

The Unitarian Templom of Meszko, 1931.

Journey's End, Life's Beginning

After two years apart, I was finally in the same country as my fiancé. I reached his native city of Kolozsvár in Transylvania just as day was breaking. It had been a seven-month journey for me, leaving California in January of 1929 and traveling through Japan, China, Russia, and finally Romania. Journey's end, for the time being. While rattling over the cobblestone streets of Kolozsvár in an ancient *fiacre*—a funny coach—I saw through the fading dark a sign that set my heart pounding: *Unitarius Kollegium*. Feri's college, where I would meet him.

I found accommodations across the street at a tiny hostel with a yawning wooden portal. An effusive chambermaid with a huge key opened the door to a minute bedroom. She patted my cheek, exclaiming in German *schone* (beautiful) and *huebsch* (good-looking), while remaining to stare at me and fondle every garment I took off.

Despite my anticipation, I slept soundly until ten o'clock. When I awoke, I skipped breakfast, dressed, and crossed the street, mounting the steps to the Kollegium with a heart that wouldn't keep quiet. My first impression of the college's bleakness never changed: endless, Kafkaesque, high-ceilinged halls that displayed portrait after portrait of scowling dignitaries with beards and walrus mustaches.

A pleasant-faced, blue-eyed young man rounded a corner. On hearing me ask for Balázs Ferenc (in Hungary, last names are pronounced first), he beamed, exclaiming in welcome English, "You are Kriszti from America!" Then he suddenly sobered. "But I suppose you know that Feri is in the hospital."

Tuberculosis, I feared; the trouble of his childhood. What would happen? At least months of rest, I was sure. As for what would happen to us, I was not as sure.

At that moment Feri's friend, Alex St. Ivanyi (Sanyi), came along. Seeing me standing in the college foyer completely at a loss, he gathered me up with an inviting smile. "Come home with me. Olga will be anxious to see you."

Sanyi, the Unitarian minister of Kolozsvár, brought me, baggage and all, to their home. Like Feri, Sanyi had ventured to bring an American wife to Transylvania. They lived in a typical Kolozsvár row house, its whitewashed front rising straight up from the dusty sidewalk. One got a glimpse of green grass in their private courtyard when the gate—a mammoth one for wagons and a small door for people—swung open.

Olga welcomed me like a long-lost sister. They had a beautiful three-year-old daughter, Eve, born in Transylvania; a second child was on the way. Olga was leaving soon to have the baby born in America, to exempt it from the horror of two years of Romanian military training should it be a boy. She had kept her American citizenship at a fee of $30 annually, a cost devastating to most Hungarian incomes.

After lunch, Sanyi took me to see the Unitarian bishop—my second shock of the day. Accustomed to the democratic spirit of American Unitarianism, I was ill prepared to step back into what felt like stuffy Victorianism. My naive belief in the inevitability of historical progress was shaken. It was only the beginning.

The bishop was a flustered old gentleman who could not seem to fit me into his landscape. He kept patting me vaguely on the head, and although he knew English, only muttered a litany of "Well, well. Dear, dear."

At four o'clock I found Feri in the third-class ward of the Romanian State Hospital. Against a white pillow, his dark, wide eyes looked larger than I remembered, his mouth more sensitive, his chin as stubborn as ever. Feri beamed at my familiar raincoat from Berkeley. For the first few days of our reunion we were shy and constrained. Then the intangible barriers broke and we knew we were as much in love as ever.

While waiting for Feri to recover, my thoughts slipped back three years to the first time I mentioned Feri to my Aunt Isabel. One day, with some hesitation, I waylaid her and fished a scrap of a poem from my notebook. I watched anxiously as she read Feri's vivid, Magyar-colored English.

The Flower

Everybody knows that love is a flower,
But do you know what a flower is?

A tiny seed in the beak of a white bird:
Does the white bird know what it is to become
When she drops it into the garden of my heart?
Wee leaves and a tender stem:
Do unwitting rain and aimless wind
Know for what they grow it in the midst of overgrowing weed?
Fragrance and pale blue petals:
do cold nights and bleak dawns
know why they freeze it to death?

Aunt Isabel exclaimed with dismay when she first saw Feri, hatless in the rain, a thin figure in a loose raincoat. With its shock of Indian-black hair, his head seemed too large for his body, and his brown eyes (were they not so interestingly set apart) too large for his head.

There was something about Feri that was forlorn and wistful, something that made me long to gather him close, gather him in. But he seemed prepossessed and austere, yet passionately wrapped up in his ideas and plans to improve the villages of his native land. Transylvania . . . Pennsylvania? . . . flashed across my provincial mind. No, "the Switzerland of Southern Europe, where the high Carpathians of old Romania come down in hills, merging with the flat plain of Hungary," said the books I dug out of the university library.

Feri was born in Kolozsvár, Transylvania, on October 24, 1901. His family came from Szekely-Keresztur, a region where the Unitarian religion first took root in the sixteenth century. The earliest church records of the Balázs family were in Csehetfalva, in 1602. When the Romanians first took over Transylvania after World War I, Feri's father, a postal official, refused to give a public oath of allegiance to Romania. After losing his job and home, he moved his family to Hungary and studied at the university, earning a doctor of law degree.

As a youth, Feri showed talent in music, writing, and art. During World War I, he contracted tuberculosis and spent two years recovering in a remote mountain village. Then he graduated from the Unitarian Theological College in Kolozsvár on scholarship. He received a scholarship from the British Unitarians for graduate study at Manchester College, Oxford, and two years at the Unitarian College in Berkeley, California, where he received a ThD degree. We met at Berkeley, where I studied social science and Feri theology.

Aunt Isabel didn't know that I had begun to dally in the streets where Feri walked, that once I stared at a plume of smoke, russet from the setting sun, not "seeing" Feri until he was beside me. I had not told her that one day I entered the unaccustomed darkness of a church and sank into a pew, limp with sudden panic that Feri might return to Transylvania without me. I prayed that I might go along.

In Feri I found a partner for my social idealism. While studying at Antioch College, I had developed a keen desire to be on the essential frontiers of our time—human relations and social institutions. Though we debated for hours, in Feri's religious convictions I found relief from my extreme scientific methodology. As a social science major at Berkeley, I had been taught to see "strictly objective" observation as primary, without regard for values. Yet it was my nature to be concerned with values. In Feri's dynamic person, however, I found no gaps between belief, knowledge, and action.

My husband as a student at the Unitarian College, Berkeley, California.

Although slight, Feri seemed tireless, always absorbed in something—composing music, writing children's stories, playing with the college printing press, or working on his philosophy of religion. The latter pursuit brought him an offer of another graduate fellowship, this time at Harvard University. But instead of further academic work, Feri decided to make a firsthand study of village life in Asia before returning home.

On January 8, 1927, I received another poem from Feri.

I want to tell you what by this time, you too
must have discovered. The little seed that fell
from the white bird's beak has grown
into a gorgeous flower. I want you to know this.
But I am full of doubts as to what the fate
of this flower will be.

Not because I have any doubts about the flower.
The flower is there; its scent spreads all over my room
and sweetens my dreams. And it has its roots laid deep.
It did not sprout up in a night's time.
It was not born of a fever that came quickly and may pass
away quickly. I have no doubts about the flower.

Nor am I full of doubts because I do not know what I want to do.
My friend has clearly spoken for me.
I want you to be my companion for a life.
I want you to come with me to Transylvania.

My doubts are about what you will and should decide.
Was it your life purpose to leave friends, relatives,
and a whole country behind you
and choose another language, another country,
another set of culture, traditions and ideals?
Have you ever thought, daughter of a rich and advanced country,
of going as a pioneer
among people that are intelligent, good willed and art-loving,
yet devoid of the advantages of civilization and of a higher culture?

I want you to answer me when your answer is ready.
Tomorrow, if your answer will be ready tomorrow.
Next month or next season, if it takes that long
to find out what the seed has become in your heart. . . .

I thought I had already spoken to you
about everything that occupied and interested my thinking,
of all the great causes to which I am devoted,
the troubles that visit me and the hobbies that cheer me up,
as white sails cheer up the morose sea.
Like an old street singer, I thought I had already sung all my melodies.
But now I see that I was quite mistaken. . . .

Deciding to say "yes" took some time. "If Feri is to be a Unitarian minister, would I fit into the role of minister's wife?" was a large question. In Transylvania, as in the early days of America, the church was the center of community life and education. I had not known that there was a Unitarianism older than my American version, one that began in 1579 when Francis David, a Hungarian, was martyred. But, finally, Feri triumphantly announced, "I have engaged Miss Frederiksen."

Our worlds began to come together. His Old World was becoming my new world. My only sorrow was that those dearest to me, especially my Aunt Isabel and Uncle Mellen, might not understand my deep desire and think me rash and foolish. I came from a Danish and American background. Born on October 3, 1903, in Chicago, I moved with my family to Minneapolis when I was five years old. My father, Ditlev Monrad Frederiksen grew up in Denmark and graduated from Harvard University and Law School. He was a man of great Danish reserve and delighted in nature and public affairs. At an early age, I accompanied him to hear outstanding social and political thinkers such as Jane Addams, Lincoln Steffens, and Upton Sinclair when they spoke at the Unitarian church in Minneapolis.

My father met my mother, Helen Williams Brown, while she was living in Paris. Lively and intelligent, she studied painting in France and Italy under James McNeil Whistler and others. She had grown up in New England, reputedly of Mayflower descent. After a twenty-year struggle with cancer, my mother died in 1927. Her youngest sister Isabel became a mother to me during the years she took care of us.

The Danish half of me was attracted to Feri's ambition—to see Transylvania move toward economic security through the kind of cooperative organization that had lifted Denmark onto its feet after its war in 1864 with Austria and Prussia. My American half—the pioneer or missionary in me—wanted to rush to the rescue of a politically downtrodden people. As for my undivided heart, it just wanted to sing and dance.

At the time I met Feri, I was finishing up at the University of California at Berkeley when I suddenly took ill with tubercular pleurisy (a result of swimming in icy water). I graduated while in the infirmary. Then I spent a couple of months recuperating in Taos, New Mexico, home of my Aunt Marie and Uncle Walter. When Feri came to visit me there, I wanted to accompany him to Asia and Europe, and tried to earn the necessary money by selling books door-to-door. No luck! I ended up teaching in the Cottage School in Hayward, then in the Peninsula School of Creative Education in Menlo Park, California.

Feri left alone for Asia. Two years later, our roles were reversed and I was to find him in the hospital bed.

I wrote home to reassure Aunt Isabel of Feri's health. "In January Feri may receive the appointment that he especially wants, a beautiful village on a mountain top, which should be a good climate for him. If at that time he must still remain in bed, an assistant will hold the position for him until he is able to take it. The doctors are considering giving him a treatment, which seems to be very popular here. Feri's case is 'benevolent' and they are going to observe him longer, before taking further steps. Don't be alarmed. The x-ray shows quite an area in his left lung, but the doctor says that with the right care now, he will recover and have a long life of activity. . . .

"Feri is an adorable person; I don't know anyone else like him. Looking squarely at all possibilities for happiness and hardship, I can only say right now that I can't imagine my life without him. But as my usefulness to him for the next few months cannot amount to much, I shall do my waiting in Denmark. PS: I am well; my survival quality is, I think, adaptability!"

As usual, Feri was oblivious to his own comfort. Third-class food was slim to start with, and he had been leaving on his tray not only meat but everything he suspected had been cooked with lard. Olga let me cook for him in her kitchen. As his inflamed lungs improved, Feri was allowed to dress and sit outdoors with me an hour every morning and afternoon.

Shopping for Feri's needs under the tutelage of Sanyi and Olga naturally introduced me to Hungarian culture. I learned important words and phrases such as *totott kapaszta* (stuffed cabbage) and *kezit csokolom* (I kiss your hand). I marveled at Olga chattering to Eve in that impossible language, putting her mammoth featherbeds to air in the windows over the street in the Hungarian manner, and driving shrewd bargains with market women ensconced among piles of onions and green peppers.

"How much?" Olga would ask, extending her cup to an open jug of sour cream.

"Twenty *lei*, my soul."

"My cup is small; I'll give you eight."

"Not possible, my heart. It's sweet and fresh—try some," responded the vendor, offering to pour a bit into her open palm.

"Ten lei," Olga bargained.

"Twelve, my dear; make it just twelve."

"If you're an American, they think you're an heiress," said Olga, as we walked from the prefect offices to the secret police to report my presence. Sanyi was still under suspicion because he was a Hungarian who had been abroad. Every now and then, the Romanian police came to search his books and papers. Olga told me how the Unitarian church, fearing the stimulus of new ideas, withheld opportunity from men who were home from study in England and America. If the young were kept waiting, more pension funds would be available to the elder clergy.

Thus Feri had not been given a church when he returned to Kolozsvár, but was put on trial in a boys' school in Cristur, a nearby town. For living quarters he was provided a room in the school basement, with a floor of loose boards over damp earth. Despite the conditions, Feri proved his character and ability. The boys found in him a new kind of teacher. No sharp, sudden box on the ears. He spoke to them as equals, and suggested that the principal do away with the school "prison." Feri told me about the prototypical lesson on good manners. Teacher: "Why should we knock before entering a door?"

"Because God wants it!" came the correct answer in a shout.

Feri had bought a projection lantern with his meager $5 monthly salary. With it he organized an adult education program, tramping from village to village in his thin coat, lugging the heavy equipment.

I was indignant and sick at heart. I wrote to Isabel, "The group who governs the church here consists of extremely narrow-minded, conservative old men. But [Feri] has stood the test. Even the silly old bishop had to 'commend' the splendid work Feri has done with the young people of the neighboring villages. . . . The longer

I know that boy the more I admire him. He carries out his social ideals and plans with a resolution and skill that is not common.

"My impression of this Unitarian church is that it has served its usefulness; it is now degenerate and corrupt. Its only use now is that it serves as a shell, in the face of Romanian aggressions, for the Hungarians to live within. However, it is not completely devoid of possibilities, the greatest being simply the opportunity for associating with people.

"I do not love this country. Conditions here are decidedly bum, but even that has its fascination. Each of these South European countries teaches its children a nationalistic legend to prove its own supremacy. They must develop a new attitude toward one another, and this can best be done, I believe, by a study of history in the scientific spirit. I sometimes wonder what curious Fate has brought me here, and how it is going to turn out."

One day I went to see Dr. Pap Livius, Feri's genial Romanian physician. Dr. Livius eyed me pityingly. "Balázs must never marry, and never have children," he said.

I did not know what to think nor which way to turn. Thus far my presence, if measured by the diminishing mercury line on Feri's thermometer, was beneficial. We agreed, though, that I should proceed with my plans to attend the Progressive Education Congress in Denmark and visit my relatives.

I had been too preoccupied with Feri's recovery to pay much attention to the pros and cons of a future life in this country. Before leaving for Denmark, I had a glimpse of the Transylvanian villages. Feri was to leave the hospital for the purer air of a mountaintop at a cottage owned by one of his professors, Dr. Kiss Elek—a fine man with a dark, keen face and a tannic acid-tinge to his spirit.

On the way to Dr. Kiss's house we stopped at Kenos, a Unitarian parish that might soon be open to a new minister. "The name Kenos means 'place of suffering'," explained Feri. "In the olden days, robbers were executed here." I fell in love with the old Kenos *templom* (church), its wooden bell tower standing aloof from the main building. Up among the bells, we looked down upon the mingled rooftops and trees, gathered protectively about the church.

"They seem tiny and lonely," I said, looking out across a treeless expanse of fields to another spire pushing up through a similar cluster of color on the horizon. An involuntary shiver moved through me, as I imagined the scene below blanketed in snow.

The old minister's wife at Kenos showed me the remote privy, the outdoor, igloo-type baking oven, and the well with its stone-weighted sweep pointing skyward.

A couple had been able to live there with about twenty-four acres for cultivation, some old fruit trees, and the villagers providing their firewood. The Romanian government paid them a salary of about $18 a month (3,000 lei). Travel, books, and luxuries were out on such a salary. "We'll write our own books," said Feri optimistically.

"How long do you want to live in a village, Feri?" I asked.

"Oh, two or three years—long enough to know what the needs are. Eventually I'd like to teach at the Kollegium. No one has a right to teach ministers without having lived as they must live."

Feri's dearest desire was to live in a peasant village, enter fully into its life, understand its needs from everyday experience over a long period of time. He challenged the use of theory alone to meet the problems of the farmers. "It is not enough to lecture to the villages," he contended. "One must be willing to forego the advantages of town life, cast one's lot with the peasants, and gradually create from within."

Living in Kolozsvár appealed to me, however. Perhaps I could qualify to teach English in the university, which had been taken over by the Romanians. We could have a hearth where the students of all sorts—Romanians, Hungarians, Germans, and Jews—could freely discuss some of the problems that were brooding bitterness among groups and individuals in the area.

The journey to Dr. Kiss's mountaintop, beautiful as it was, unfortunately brought a rise in Feri's temperature. We reached the small unfinished cottage, a haven above a troubled countryside. Although living conditions were simple, they were adequate. Every night for supper there was a hunk of stiff *polizska* (boiled cornmeal mush served on a board and cut in slices with a string) and buffalo milk. Feri's outdoor reclining chair looked up into the towering and dissolving clouds and out over hills that rolled away like a green ocean.

There on the mountain, I reluctantly left him.

En route to Denmark, I stopped to see friends in Czechoslovakia. Americans were popular there in 1929, perhaps because US President Wilson had helped to bring Czechoslovakia's several groups into an uneasy national partnership. Although its minorities seemed to be receiving fairer treatment than in Romania, some tensions were reported.

In Copenhagen I found a refreshingly vital international spirit. At the conference in Helsingor, teachers from many countries mingled together in a spirit of departure from the past and the promise of happier prospects for children. All the while, though, I kept thinking of Feri in his very different environment. "Transylvanian children are like American children," I mused. "After all, does it matter where one person casts her lot?"

The visit to Denmark was a surprisingly personal odyssey. I wrote to my father, "Such a blooming countryside and pretty red-tile roofed houses, and leisurely, kindly people. . . . I am living at Aunt Karen's villa at Snekkersten. Peter and Emmy Louisa Manniche of the International People's College are dears. Even though I knew she was my second cousin, I thought of them as *your* relatives rather than my own. I did not imagine that they would mean any more to me than other interesting people. So it was quite a wonderful and unexpected experience to discover, with some of them, an immediate kinship and understanding. . . . I felt it a compliment when they decided that I was 'a Frederiksen,' although well I know how I must always be on guard against certain Frederiksen traits: more interests than one human being can possibly accomplish in one lifetime, with resultant lack of concentration."

In late August came an SOS from Feri, insisting that I come back to Hungary as soon as possible. "I can't get well without you!" he said. Obsessed by his vision and plans, would Feri ever pay proper attention to his physical needs without my care and support?

I returned to Feri via Budapest to meet his family. "How will I get along with your mother when I don't know her language?" I had asked Feri cautiously.

"You'll get along for that very reason!" he laughed.

As for Feri's father, as long as there were people around, hardship could not touch him. I loved him right away. My future parents-in-law had gifts for us, and by their impressive enunciation of the words "svetaire" and "pairls," I recognized the sacrifice such purchases represented. A sweater was badly needed by Feri . . . but pearls for me? His parents' saving from their tiny pension to provide Feri with a heavy overcoat and minister's gown brought home to me the oppressive necessity of material things.

When I visited a progressive school in Budapest and saw the minute, cramped drawings of the children, I remarked, "In America, they make large pictures with big brushes to get a sense of freedom and sweep."

"We don't have the paper," the principal replied.

The post-war poverty of Budapest was evident. In a city crowded with refugees from minority areas, work was scarce. My perspectives were becoming reshuffled. Breakfasts of chicory coffee and plain bread left me feeling undernourished. Little things filled me with jarring apprehension, such as gold caps on people's teeth, walrus mustaches, enormous high-ceilinged rooms, walls with overpowering stenciled patterns, large ornate furniture, and mammoth cupboards into which everything had to be squeezed. I hated myself for such feelings, and for being preoccupied with what was, after all, trivia.

But other things compensated. Feri's sister Ibolyka at the piano and her husband Bandi, with his violin, made their apartment ring with Bach and Beethoven. Ibolyka sang in the Budapest Grand Opera, and took me with her to rehearsals.

Budapest was breathtaking. Steep and narrow cobbled streets and ancient, palace-covered hills of Buda contrasting with the modern factories of industrial Pest; the flight of strong yet airy bridges across the Danube River; the incomparable stone dignity and exquisite beauty of the Houses of Parliament reflected in the water. But the beautiful buildings along the Danube mostly belonged to the past. I spent ten days in that city of interesting monuments—mostly military memories of repulsed invasions. In the central square were four new and terrible monuments of ferocious warriors, each in an attitude of defense over the prostrate body of a woman. Each symbolized one of the four frontier regions taken away by the Treaty of Trianon and given to Czechoslovakia, Romania, Yugoslavia, and Austria. I met Hungarians who were grimly determined to recover these territories, even if it took a few centuries. Every day, schoolchildren repeated a prayer to this effect.

Denmark had exalted Woodrow Wilson for advocating the self-determination of peoples and opposing the division of defeated nations. Now I felt the heavy burden of the treaty that had reduced both the territory and population of Hungary by more than half. It seemed a barbarous thing—the deliberate division of a country—handing over millions of people to a strange rule, language, education, and tyranny.

"The culture of the country is Hungarian. All the city and town regions with schools and other institutions are Hungarian," I wrote to Father. "If the Romanians slightly outnumbered Hungarians, they were peasants who sifted into the country as serfs. The Szekler-Hungarians of Transylvania never were serfs, and developed self-government to a remarkable degree. Transylvania now shows most conspicuously the deteriorating effect of a government run by an (as yet) incapable people."

True to their fiery temperament, Hungarians dramatized the situation. Flags were flown at half mast and flowers planted in patriotic designs. Everywhere in big letters was the slogan, *Nem, nem, soha!* (No, no, never!) A prayer posted in public places and recited daily by schoolchildren was:

I believe in one god.
I believe in one country.
I believe in one eternal justice.
I believe that the Fatherland will be resurrected.

At first the rabid nationalism seemed incredible. But just as incredible was the irresponsibility of the Allied governments in putting entire populations under alien rule, without sufficient respect for history and cultural autonomy. Contrary to agreements under the League of Nations, the Romanians had in effect confiscated Hungarian high schools, universities, libraries, museums, and hospitals, replacing Hungarian personnel with Romanians without compensation. Because of the intentionally difficult Romanian University entrance examination, eighty percent of the Hungarian students flunked it. Unable to enter the university built by their ancestors, they were becoming manual workers.

Back in Transylvania, I moved with Feri to recuperate at a parsonage in the tiny village of Homorod Ujfalu. Our host there was Dobai Pista, village minister and former classmate of Feri, and his wife Irenka.

Pista was the type of emotional Hungarian characterized by an oft-repeated phrase, *a mi lelkunk* (our own souls). He seemed to see God through a glowing dust cloud of personal drama. In Transylvania, where the means of living were simple and visibly related to the ends, such young men as Pista weren't geared to a complex economic machine. Instead, they wrote. They were anxious about their style and how they related to poets, historians, and religious leaders. Feri also was deeply aware of himself in a poetic way. To cast his lot with a village, he wrote, was like sowing himself "under the clod." "Will I come up, will I flower and bear fruit?" Feri asked.

Despite his poetic nature, Pista tried to regulate the morals of Homorod Ujfalu with medieval simplicity. He publicly scolded girls who became unexpectedly pregnant, expelling them from church until public apology was made.

In my letter home, I told Isabel the village school at Homorod Ujfalu was "bare, rough, without equipment. When the minister gives a little 'moral' preachment to the youngsters, I take one of my lovely Russian picture books to show them, and they go wild with delight. Charming children, they are so eager and unspoiled, tiny men and women in tattered homespun clothes, long trousers and long full skirts, just like their fathers and mothers.

"I want very much to have an art class with them once or twice a week, but they have no materials. If you feel so inclined, I'd very much appreciate one or two dozen boxes of crayons. . . . It would be fascinating . . . to see what children like these who have nothing and have seen nothing, would do. . . .

"I am satisfied with Feri's improvement. . . . He goes up on top of the hill twice a day, and stretches out in his steamer chair. It is glorious up there, looking over fields of literally golden grain and hills of russet forest. He is writing (too much, I think). . . .

"This is the order of the day. The maid, Maria, builds a fire in the little iron stove. I get up, dress, put the room in order. It is now quite a cozy, homelike room. I threw out various red plush articles of furniture and wish I could throw out the gigantic ugly wardrobes! . . . With all your books about, a dish of fruit, a vase of autumn flowers, and you and Uncle Mellen on the desk, it is very attractive.

"Feri comes in and stretches out in his steamer chair. I go out and scale a high ladder for great bunches of grapes. We breakfast on milk, bread, butter and honey, and scrambled eggs. Ordinarily, people don't eat much butter here. It is put on the table as a special treat. Then I chop kindling . . . sweep the room, take Feri's chair on top of the hill, and remain there for an hour talking, reading, or writing. Come down, get our dinner. . . . Irenka said I leaned over the stove as though I were reading a book! But now I have proved myself. After dinner, rest. At 4:30, milk and bread and butter for both of us. Then we study Hungarian on the hilltop and enjoy the marvelous colors of the hills as the sun goes down. Supper, then I mend clothes (!!!). And so to bed."

Irenka had warned me at length on what it was like to be a *Tiszteletes Asszony* (minister's wife) in those out-of-the-way hills. The difficulties of daily living were almost beyond her endurance. The bus to town was three bumpy hours by wagon and 75 lei. She tramped out her loneliness in the company of a dog, maintained an undaunted polish on her monumental furniture, and cooked to perfection the traditional Hungarian dishes, with endless chopping of onions and parsley and rolling of sheets of noodles.

Like other *uri* (gentlewomen), Irenka wore a cluster of enormous keys to lock every cupboard the moment she removed the least sugar lump or rag. *Lopjak mint a tuz.* (They steal like fire.) Her Hungarian townperson's facility for berating a servant or villager left me aghast. "If I find it so hard, what is it going to be like for you, all the way from America?" she asked.

I wrote to Aunt Isabel, "The Hungarian villages are primitive, poor, and forlorn beyond my imagination. . . . There is something about the peasants, though, that appeals to me. In the course of the next months I hope to know this little village in which we are living, and get some idea of the possibilities of a folk high school. . . .

"Feri lies just beside the wall in his chair, and I lean against an old tombstone now, writing. . . . I puzzle out the often blurred inscriptions on these old stone slabs or we build up a conversation about the world around us or memorize poems of the great Hungarian poet, Petofi, or plug through the French Hungarian grammar. It is a remarkably difficult language. Feri says he cares more for me than for Transylvania, so if I find that I cannot be happy here, he will go somewhere else!"

Feri was getting stronger. During those autumn afternoons, we would climb to the hilltop cemetery to look down on tiny yellowing fields, shaved tidily as though by a barber. Soon the air took on a chill, a forewarning of winter closing down over the village and fields and forests beyond. Then came the vast blanket of whiteness, no ordinary snow, it seemed, covering countless isolated villages and turning them in on themselves, antlike, consuming their small stores.

Pista had been roaming the fields and courtyards to make sure the parishioners had not forgotten their tithes of wood and wheat for the church. Irenka had stored *krumpli* (potatoes) and *kapszta* (cabbage) in the cellar. The price of buffalo milk rose several lei a quart. We were glad to buy sacks of hazelnuts and a carved wooden nutcracker from some Romanian mountain lads. Hens stopped laying so an egg for Feri became worth its weight in gold. Daily I tramped the length of the village from door to door, thankful if the yield was one egg. Because his lungs suffered from the cold, I developed a priestess's attitude toward the fire in Feri's little iron stove.

One day I remembered the donkey-skin puppets I had purchased in China on my way to Transylvania, and unearthed from my suitcase the troop of brightly colored little people, horses, wild animals, and even a dragon. The figures were translucent enough for a lamp placed behind a stretched curtain to shine through them. Feri and I made up stories for the little acting company, constructing scenery out of larded paper. It would be hard to say who was the most enthusiastic in these productions—Feri and I, Pista and Irenka, who helped stage the performances, or the villagers who came to watch.

About this time, Pap Livius—the doctor who had told Feri never to marry—came forth with an opinion that he was making a remarkable recovery. But at about the same time, we found that we could not get married, because of a discrepancy between the laws of Romania and the United States. Romania required a document that the American consulate had no authority to give. It felt like a foolish, bitter, bureaucratic game. I traveled to Bucharest to appeal to higher-ups on both sides.

I told my Aunt Grace, "We have written, translated, and paid for numerous documents from local prefects, American consuls, and the Romanian ministry in Bucharest. When I wrote to the American consulate asking what on earth a person could do, this very evening I receive this brief and enlightening reply: 'The Consulate is pleased to furnish the following information: Marriage should be performed in accordance with the requirements of the Romanian marriage laws.'

"However, we manage to somehow enjoy the situation simply because the Unitarian dignitaries take it so solemnly. Poor things; it's just a 'moral crisis' in their otherwise uneventful existence. The old bishop would adore to say some hokus-pokus over us to set us right, but he doesn't dare. He's a minority bishop and cannot risk saying a word until the proper legal preliminaries are gone through with."

In Bucharest, I learned that I came out on the right side of one law that permitted me to keep my American citizenship without frequent and expensive trips across the Atlantic. Frustrated, I finally gave over to the wide boulevards and splendid new buildings of the city. Making up for lost time, Bucharest seemed to be trying to qualify as a full-fledged European capital in half a generation. I admired the magnificent state opera, yet felt pain that it was supported by a tax that could have more than cared for the poor roads and minority schools of Transylvania or improved Romanian villages.

"We are lucky that they aren't paying too much attention to us Transylvanian Hungarians," Feri said. "It gives us time to lay our own groundwork."

It seemed advisable for us to spend the winter in a larger place. While I was in Bucharest, Feri scouted out the town of Szekler Keresztur. On a side street of crooked little houses with fringes of yellow corn under their eaves, he found a room and a kitchen, with another room across the courtyard, all for 500 lei—little more than $3 per month. "Kitchen" was a euphemism for the cubby with a low stovehole for a door, on which I repeatedly banged my head. Feri's imagination took him on a shopping tour to piece out a few furnishings, including a stunning embroidered Saxon tablecloth, lovely peasant pottery, and the essential *mak mag* or poppyseed grinder.

Feri's idea of resting was to launch a magazine, *Keves Kotes*, just for peasant youth, especially those from the 120 Unitarian Szekely villages. We had fun creating linoleum block illustrations for the magazine, and were excited when poems, plays, and even critical articles began flowing to us from the boys and girls.

Feri did other interesting things while recuperating, including educational lantern-slide lectures. We hoped the first lantern equipment would eventually produce enough profit to buy ten others, so that the next year every village would have a program every two weeks. We hoped by the end of the year there would be a $2,500 to $3,000 profit to devote to beginning a folk high school. The school would be a small community of work and study, mainly self-supporting, with its own dairy and gardens; and the students would earn something at such industries as furniture, carved and colored in peasant style, and a printing press. We conjured dreams of making a beautiful series of pictures on Transylvania to show in America to earn money for the folk high school.

Feri also arranged a conference for young people—three days of study and friendship. These projects were truly exciting because they were breaking new ground in that part of the world.

"One must devise ways of getting around its stupid and unjust regulations," I exploded to Isabel. "For example, we cannot sell 'tickets' for the lantern lectures or thirty-three percent of the profit must go to the Romanian state. . . . Or when paying a government tax . . . you don't automatically receive a receipt, you must *pay a further tax* to get a receipt, otherwise you're apt to be requested to pay your first tax over and over again!"

We went into debt to buy a gloriously illustrated new edition of the *Encyclopedia Britannica*. Feri wanted both pictures and material for more lantern-slide programs. What a sensation the encyclopedia created in Transylvania! For years, it was the library to which our village turned for everything from curiosity about foreign sheep raising to skepticism about bacteria.

"Feri is away in the 'city' nearby, seeing the third number of the paper into print," I wrote to Isabel. "The things we write together have a way of surprising us. . . . We build on one another's ideas with much livelier results than either of us could reach alone. . . . We have to use the few resources we have, even if they are crude, but it is the only thing in the way of 'education' these youths of 120 villages have. They do appreciate it, and are sending us more and more of their own attempts.

"As for freedom of thought, which is supposedly a Unitarian attribute, in our paper a boy of eighteen . . . characterized a play written by one of the elders of the church as 'conventional' and 'mediocre.' A just judgment! But that it should be said! And by a youth! The central office of the church let us know that they were 'shocked.' Such old duffers! After they've had their few years of theological study, they go to a little village and stagnate for the rest of their lives, with no subsequent freshening of ideas."

In such a small, remote community, Feri and I decided we should invest in wedding rings. Brass was all we could afford. We wore the rings decorously on the street and when we got back to our quarters, we took them off and hung them on a nail on the wall.

While waiting for our assignment to a parish, Feri and I took off for Bucharest at the end of January 1930. "As we journeyed across the great plain on the Romanian side of the Carpathians," I wrote home, "Feri and I were amazed at the poverty of the Romanian villages. They were much worse off than the Transylvanians. I cannot completely share the Hungarians' bitter condemnation. Considering the Romanians' past, their recent liberation from Turkish oppression, and still more recent shaking off of their own utterly corrupt and absolute political power, I think they have done well.

"Mr. Maniu, leader of the Peasant Party now in control, is a man of devotion and principles. He has cleaned out much rottenness and most of what remains can be changed only by slow education. There are so many problems affecting immediate Romanian welfare that the outlying troubles of the minorities cannot be touched for perhaps several years. Feri believes this to be fortunate, as it allows leeway for building up strong general opinion and demand for the cultural autonomy of the Szeklers. He and several other young men who are recognized leaders in Transylvanian reconstruction are at work on a book discussing the prospects.

"There are incredibly few Hungarians who have a spirit of strengthening the common lot of the Transylvanians . . . and thinking of change in terms of quietly unifying . . . their own group. Either they dream in vain of reunion with Hungary by political means . . . or they incapacitate themselves by bitterness and hate. It seems to me that people are not so much the victims of social injustice, crippling as it may seem, but rather of their own dependence on their old institutions. . . .

"I talked with the American consul in Bucharest. . . . If I marry, my children have to be Romanian citizens, but I may keep my citizenship. If I were an American *man* marrying a Romanian woman, my children would be Americans! Did I once dream of a hope called 'rights for women'? . . .

"It is not easy to make my decision on marriage. Sometimes it seems as though it is not I who chose this course, but some 'Fate' beyond my control. There is a theory that 'the things that happen are essentially like the persons to whom they happen.' Certainly it is *I* who came here, who persisted in coming here. And those elements in my nature and desire seem to have been of a 'fateful,' inevitable, sort."

Feri hoped that we would end up in Szeklerland, the large island of Magyar villages in the center of Transylvania. He felt that the Szeklers would lend themselves more readily to cooperative efforts than the mixed Magyar-Romanian villages. However, the next church vacancy was not in Szeklerland, but in Meszko (mays-ker), a mixed Romanian-Hungarian village of 350 Unitarian-Hungarians and 500 Romanians. The Meszko Unitarians had just ousted their minister because he sued them for refusing to raise his low income, which had become fixed at about a dollar a year.

The Romanian government paid a salary to all ministers in its territories. The highest salary went to the state church, the Greek Orthodox, then in decreasing order to Greek Catholics, Roman Catholics, and Calvinists. Last came the Unitarians, who survived only through their strong ties with British and American Unitarians.

If we took the Meszko parish, we were told we would receive about $18 a month, or 3,000 lei. The village would supply a house, some land, and firewood. It was spring, and we were at the end of our resources. In Meszko, at least we would have a little money, soil, seeds, and a community that might become a proving ground that Hungarians and Romanians could work in harmony.

As usual, there was an obstacle. Because most of a village often descends from one family tree, there was strong support in Meszko for another candidate—a relative of most of the villagers. His father was reportedly offering drinks, promising that his son would be content with even less pay than was expected.

"No stranger would consider for a moment coming to a raggy, dirty village like this unless there was something wrong with him!" the father argued.

However, Feri won the post, which he attributed to two things. When he visited the church at Meszko he avoided "preaching." Instead, he talked informally in the school, using lantern pictures from his travels. Also, Kovacs Janos, the village school teacher or *Tanito* (second to the minister in community leadership), wanted Feri for a friend and neighbor. Kovacs was a wiry, authoritarian young man. On the night of the election, he went about the village rounding up all the old women who ordinarily did not vote, even routing some out of their beds, urging them to support Feri.

The region's Unitarian bishop confirmed the results of the election in Feri's favor. According to one of the theological professors, the bishop had approved "because it would be wise to put a young man with radical ideas in a place where the going was tough." Disquieting to me was Meskzo's reputation as an ugly village.

"But if the peasants themselves call something ugly, you'd find it full of charm," Feri argued with a wink.

Alabaster and Mud

On April 6, 1930, we headed for Meszko. Torda, the nearest town, was seven kilometers away, and the city of Kolozsvár was two hours by bus. Requisitioning an antiquated truck, we dumped the winter's dusty straw out of our mattresses and piled them on, along with the *Britannicas*, our manuscripts, cooking gear, clothes, our little kitty Macska in a pillowcase, and ourselves.

My mood was like the countryside in spring, a mixture of hope and depression. The ghost of my artist mother traveled with me. I remembered her paintings of French villages and the peasant jugs she loved so much. All along the way I saw through Mother's eyes the breathing green of Corot landscapes and Millet figures and faces. When Macska meowed from the depths, I hugged her close to my breast.

After sixteen hours and three blowouts on roads made for ox carts, we climbed the rugged Meszko hill. The minister's barn, granary, and pigsty were black hulks in the moonlight. By contrast, the whitewashed walls of the parish house gleamed a bright welcome. It was the typical four rooms in a row, with a veranda down its length. After unloading our possessions into an empty room, we made a stumbling excursion to a neighbor's haystack for straw to fill Feri's mattress.

I walked on to the Kovacs' house, where I was expected to spend the night. Feri stayed alone in the parish house. Because people in the villages were so strict in their customs, we wondered if we should have arrived unmarried. The thought of living indefinitely in separate houses—even across the street—was hard, and it was difficult for me to believe people could be so narrow.

Tiptoeing past the sleeping family, I made my way to the little guest chamber where a lamp was left burning for me. Save for bed, clothespress, and a chair, the room was barren. But as I climbed into bed, I caught sight of an alabaster vase in a corner on the floor. I delighted in its soft, white-veined marble, which absorbed the lamplight with a subdued and mellow glow. The house in which I slept and, indeed, the "dirty" village of Meszko rested upon a hillside of alabaster, one of the choice alabaster deposits in the world.

In the Kovacs' living room, surrounded by the customary beds, we breakfasted the next morning on cups of hot milk and dark brown bread. The table was covered with a home-woven hemp cloth, like harsh linen. The loom that had woven it was clacking away in the kitchen. Encouraged by my enthusiasm, Kovacs' sister Etelka, a gentle girl with high cheekbones and oblique eyes, brought out her winter's weaving. "There's always work," she sighed.

At the kitchen table an old woman was laboriously sorting beans from a heap of hulls and earth. Meszko was close enough to Torda and Kolozsvár to have passed beyond the primitive stages of productivity and art, but it was remote enough to be weighed down by dawn-to-dark drudgery. Etelka's sewing machine, the only one in the village, stood out smartly against the splintery floor, the little iron stove, and the thick white crockery.

In a dark corner I discovered a chest with its date of 1700 and flower-painted surfaces worn all but invisible. In the living room was a heavy carved bookcase of the same age. It had formerly served as the village library, but in recent times had been banished, along with its books, from the Romanian-controlled school.

I walked down the hill to Feri. By daylight, the parish house looked old and plain but of nice proportions. The interior was rather dark because of a long veranda and no windows on the opposite side. The kitchen was like the Kovacs', an iron stove and a splintery floor worn into hollows, in places through to the earth below. However, with two southern windows it was the most pleasant room in the house. From the kitchen I could see the whole sweep of the Aranyos (golden) Valley, with its river like a silvery skein of yarn, separating sometimes into strands, winding around another village about three kilometers away, and on to the distant smokestacks of Torda.

Feri had filled the bookshelves and was arranging Japanese prints on the wall. We had no furniture other than our two cots, so I began to arrange the packing boxes together and lay out our few pots and spoons. Macska, bent on discovery, crawled inside the tall brown-tiled stove.

Our first climb around the village had the wonder of a child's first Christmas tree excursion. The air was filled with the tremulous call of newborn goats and lambs. Although the name Meszko means "limestone," in reality it was alabaster, thrust up here and there into the weather, like mountains in a Chinese painting. Meszko was a wayward village, with paths and roads winding over and around outcroppings of the pinkish-blue rock. A sunlit haze of flowering fruit trees partially obscured three hundred shaggy-thatched, brown-shingled, and red-tile roofed houses huddled above the river. Woven willow fences and walls of alabaster boulders reiterated the curves of the hillside in a downward dance, and set tiny patches of courtyards, orchards, and gardens against each other in rhomboids and trapezoids.

The farmers, with their love of level ground, cursed the alabaster. "*A fene egyen meg!* (May a loathsome disease eat it away!)" they yelled. Yet some mined their own yards for the soft, lovely stone. Every day, buffalo wagons loaded with alabaster crept out across the plain to the plant in Torda.

Dominating the scene was the Romanian church, a modern edifice of cement and tin roof, its homely t-square accuracy the sign of a small-town builder. It was built on land the Unitarian Hungarians had been saving for their new church. The 350 Unitarians of Meszko still worshiped in the fifteenth-century templom, a quaint little whitewashed church with a wooden bell tower that was sinking dangerously on one side. The villagers had been saving money to rebuild it with a modern addition. Feri thought he could persuade them to restore the ancient church in keeping with its heritage. Restoring it would leave a large sum of the accumulated funds, enough to build a badly needed community house.

One day on our way home we stopped to admire a huge flowering jasmine bush. An earth-colored figure, at first almost invisible, straightened up from her onion sets to clasp and kiss our hands through the fence that separated us. "*Lelkem! Szivem!* (My soul, my heart!)" she exclaimed, first to a somewhat startled Feri, then to me. The woman was Jula Neni, one of the poorest women in the village and one of the most intelligent. She became from that moment our devoted friend. In Hungarian, *neni* means aunt. Although we later acquired many black-kerchiefed *nenis* in the village, there was only one Jula Neni.

At first I lived across the street from Feri in the home of another benevolent, wrinkled old neni. Each dawn, through my open window I could hear a Gypsy boy pipe the village pigs out of their gates, with his translucent cow's horn. He would be followed shortly by a Magyar youth herding a stream of Hungarian cows. Then a

Romanian sounded a different note, as guardian of the goats. Those morning calls symbolized the mix of the village. They also signaled permission for me to cross the barrier of road and join my fiancé for breakfast and whatever the day had in store.

When and how could we get married? One April day shortly after we arrived, someone shouted behind us. It was the minister from a neighboring village. "You can get married!" he exclaimed. "I talked with our notary. He is an old man about to retire. He said, 'Never mind nonsensical foreign documents—after me, the deluge!' They won't bother to investigate him after he's retired. He'll tie you up tomorrow so tightly nobody can ever undo it!"

Oh, kind man, good man! A Romanian, moreover, willing to thumb his nose at technicalities for a Hungarian! Such was our legal Romanian ceremony. Soon afterward, we were married again in a proper Unitarian religious ceremony in our lovely fifteenth-century templom. The Magyars did themselves proud in their preparations. All the white lilacs of the village seemed to be massed inside the church.

My wedding gown—my pale green silk travel dress with a lacy tan vest—must have been impressive, for several village women fingered it lovingly. I carried a mammoth bouquet of white lilacs and red tulips presented by some village girls. The ceremony, in Hungarian of course, was wasted on me. I caught such phrases as "from far across the seas," and gathered that the minister considered ours one of the great loves of the ages. Although I was told that I performed my part well in Hungarian, my mind was on the letters I had received from home, my friends and family far away. When I thought of how disappointed they would be that I was taking this step, I began to weep and bent my face over my flowers.

"That's fine, that's fine," whispered Feri reassuringly, "just the right thing to do. They love an excuse for a good cry." Sure enough, from the black-kerchiefed side of the church where the married women sat, as well as from the balcony where the red-kerchiefed young women were perched, came audible sniffs and nose blowing.

I was praying with all my heart that my mother and Aunt Isabel would be wrong in their prophecies. Feri *could* take care of me, and I wished that I were wise enough to prevent or avoid their warnings. For a few moments the event seemed a nightmare and I wondered if the best thing to do might not be to sink to the floor in a pretend faint.

After the ceremony, the villagers couldn't stop doting on us. A real ordeal was coping with the one hundred kisses piled upon my "public" hand. "You'll get used to it," laughed Feri. When we returned to the *Papilak* (parsonage), there were flowers everywhere—lilacs, peonies, narcissus, tulips, and exquisite wildflowers the children had brought in from the woods. Women had made wonderful white frothy cakes. Led by the Tanito Kovacs, about sixty school children had sneaked into the parsonage ahead of us and were singing a lusty welcome. Now it could be my home, too!

As soon as I could, I withdrew to the kitchen to finish my weep. Some of the peasant women who had observed my downcast face in the church came up to greet me afterward, their eyes filled with tears. I was struck by their sweetness and fine, intelligent faces.

For a week after our wedding, gifts poured in. Barefoot women brought aprons full of eggs, jugs of buffalo milk, and plates of sheep-milk cheese. I began to think that life in this village would not be hard after all.

"Do they feel they have to propitiate your powers of priestcraft?" I teased Feri.

He quickly disillusioned me. "Every family brings something to the new *Pap* (minister). You'll be bargaining with them next week!" he laughed. Feri was right. However, the people never laughed at my struggle with their language. They became my teachers, overflowing with well-intentioned advice.

It took months for me to discover that I was no privileged character. I was deep in my dream of what Feri would accomplish, and charmed by storybook aspects of our new life. Just the new and fantastic names of things created a reality.

"From now on we'll speak only Hungarian," was a resolve we often repeated but never kept. Dealing with the simple objects of daily living in the village in Hungarian was enough; with Feri I had to speak English. His own thinking was different enough from mine and the Hungarian point of view sufficiently at odds with the American.

The dogma about a woman's place gradually bore in upon me. Food growing, gathering, cooking, and preserving took most of my time. Jula Neni and my other neighbors watched over me, partly because of my position as the Tiszteletes Asszony, but also because of my physical limitations from my earlier bout with tuberculosis.

A key word to peasant living was scarcity. Water was a scarce item in Meszko. Through rain and snow, women carried water on their heads up the hill from the Aranyos River. In the summer the river was asplash with the frog-like bodies of playing children and women cautiously scrubbing themselves against the tug of their drifting petticoats. The shore bristled with washing stools. Several weeks' accumulation of clothes were soaked at home in water poured through wood ashes, then soaped and pounded at the river and carried, wet and heavy, back up the long hill again.

When they had to break the river's winter ice to wash their clothes, the women took jugs of hot water along to keep their hands from freezing. I often met them on the road, exhausted and chilled through, their hands bleeding. No wonder I would mistake their ages. No wonder many babies were lost prematurely. As she was dying, our neighbor Klari Neni said to Feri, "Please don't let them put much earth on top of me. I've borne so many heavy things I just couldn't stand it."

Daily toil and exposure did not give peasant women sub- or superhuman endurance. Her apron full of potatoes and a basket of clay on her head, Jula Neni would exclaim, "Yoy! How tired I am. Every day it is like this."

Once I found her shivering in bed, despite a fire roaring in her stove. "The wind went through me like a knife, and it pains here," Jula Neni cried, lifting a hand to her chest. Despite my urgings that she lie down again, she shamefacedly climbed out of bed. "I have to cook some potatoes for my pig," she said stoically.

Water was a scarce item in Meszko. Several weeks' accumulation of clothes were soaked at home then soaped and pounded at the Aranyos River, which flowed below the town.

For about two months after our arrival in the village, I ran a low fever. A doctor said that one lung was slightly inflamed. A helper, Roszie, began to come for two hours a day. She hauled wood and water, washed dishes and swept. I got the meals and took care of the garden, lying down from time to time, careful not to do work that created weight for my chest. Another neighbor, sixteen-year-old Kato, came to do the heavy work.

No small part of Meszko's daily battle was with mud. After a slight rain the tenacious, gluey stuff was ankle deep or higher, except for slippery protrusions of alabaster from which one leaped, goat-fashion. Every lane was a rivulet, every step a struggle. The path from our home led downhill and across a slough of mud. Like the villagers, I wore knee-high boots. Not only an expensive necessity (worth an average month's wages), boots were works of art: handmade, with soles fastened by tiny, hand-hewn wooden pegs instead of nails, and decorated with floral insets of red leather. I finally learned to walk in a way that would not leave me, stocking foot waving helplessly in midair, hopping to retrieve a boot from the viscous mud. Almost an institution, mud was a source of much struggle and philosophy. Through the natural challenge of simply placing one foot before the other, I understood at last the fatalism of Meszko.

"*Sar van* (There is mud)," was the invariable greeting from my neighbors.

"*Sar bizony!* (Certainly, mud!)" responded I and everyone else.

Making a home in Meszko was a struggle for us. Some days I felt hopeful and content. Other days were endless questioning. Always the contradiction, the fine mixture.

To survive, we threw ourselves into small farming with all our hearts and energies. Agricultural bulletin in hand, we journeyed to an animal fair to purchase a cow. I was convinced that one should know something about the pedigree of one's purchase and see by trial and observation how much milk it would give, submit a sample of its milk to the Babcock butterfat test, and know that it had been tested for tuberculosis. I soon learned that such things were impossible in Transylvania.

Nonetheless, we handed over our last fifty dollars, walked a great black and white creature home over fifteen miles of mountains, and milked her. She turned out to be a decent, moderately hardworking cow. We named her Piros, and her calf was a darling. Whenever life grew dull, we'd say, "Come on, let's let the calf loose!" Its cavortings were a never-ending amazement and amusement to us.

"I despair of ever getting clean milk," I wrote Dr. Earl Wilbur, president of the Unitarian College in Berkeley and Feri's mentor, who had sent the agricultural bulletins. "When I read Feri's remark [to you] about our 'trying to do scientific farming,' my feelings were a mixture of amusement and despair. We are really babes in the woods! Of what use is our knowledge if we have not the means to practice it?

"The stable is filthy. I asked a villager to clean it, who, after making a few ineffectual passes at it with broom and pitchfork, said it was all right. I made an attack upon it myself but soon gave up, exhausted, choked with the dust, cobwebs, and dried manure of ages, and plentifully supplied with fleas. The floor is dirt, with a few loose rotten boards. People here make no provision for keeping manure, which accumulates in huge heaps outside the barn door. As you go along the street, you often have to step over, around, or through streams of brown ooze from these piles. Though the weather is not yet warm, swarms of flies infest the kitchen. Screens seem to be unheard of.

"Kato and her mother, who live in a little thatched house across the road, do our milking. . . . I have instituted a few simple practices, such as washing hands and washing the udders of the cow, but Feri maintains that if I insist on extending the washing to hind legs and tail, we would lose their services. At present I perform the nightly rite of holding the tail as far away from its source as possible—perhaps we can devise some better method—such as tie it to the ceiling. Rather than awaken at four o'clock in the morning to do this duty, I have contented myself with straining out great chunks of manure later, and boiling the residue."

I noticed strange lumps on our cow's back. Whenever I asked any of the villagers about it, I always got the same unsatisfying answer, "*Egeseges!*" (Good health, a sign of health and youth.) It didn't look like health to me. In perusing one of our pamphlets, I came upon a suggestion of warbles. I got scissors, hot water, and soap, and submitted poor Piros to two hours of severe treatment, being rewarded by several hard kicks and slashes in the eye from a manurey tail. At last I extracted a huge grub that grows in a cow's back from the egg of the warble fly.

"I cannot anticipate just what Kato or her mother will do next," I told Dr. Wilbur. "No sooner do I succeed in abolishing one little custom, then another, totally unexpected one turns up. They no longer milk immediately after shoveling out the barn. They no longer throw the towel with which they wash the teats across the cow's poor sick back, but just two days ago I caught the mother dipping her finger into the fresh milk and wiping it, in the form of a cross, upon the cow's back. She explains that it is an age-old custom, done by everyone in the village during every milking, to prevent the cow's milk from being 'taken away.'"

When our cow gave bloody milk, the villagers insisted it was because a swallow had flown beneath the cow! The remedy? Lay a spindle beside the cow. During the night a weasel will come and spin, and lo! next morning, the milk will be white! Once when we were unduly enthusiastic over our little calf, a wiser peasant woman quickly said, "Pth! Pth!" to help prevent the sudden destruction of something too highly praised.

Feri and I finally screwed up our courage and asked the church to put a cement floor in our barn, and build a little covered cement tank to hold the manure. We made our appeal not on the grounds of cleanliness and health, but on economy—a cement tank prevents the waste of half the manure, so why not try it as an experiment? They debated the matter with much head shaking and consideration of expense . . . perhaps in three or four years. However, since the floor needed to be repaired anyway and since cement costs no more than wood, they agreed to cement not the entire floor, but a strip running under the most economically important portion of the cow.

A cow led to a horse, so back to the animal fair. We fell in love with a tall, white, three-year-old Hungarian stallion; a stunning creature, quick and intelligent, who could run like a racehorse. We named him Jancsi. Although spirited, Jancsi was gentle and friendly. With a check from America, we bought whitewash to make decent the abode of beloved Jancsi, dutiful Piros and her calf Botsy, irrepressible Donkee, as well as the house of our aristocratic chickens: six Rhode Island Reds, ten Leghorns, and two of village breed. Our helper Rozsie filled all the cracks in the walls of the stable and the chicken house with clay and horse manure. We had to plaster the many chinks of the stable walls with mud before we whitewashed them.

At night, Feri and I enjoyed visiting our animal family by lamp light. The creatures would cease their munching and look around, expecting us to come and pet them. Feri was so fond of the creatures that I had to caution him not to be overly enthusiastic in front of certain hard-bitten peasants who might think him naive. However, one time Feri—sworn pacifist—gave Piros a beating with a big stick. She had kicked several times, sending the milk flying, and none of our new education methods had any effect on her. She must have been beaten previously, for afterwards she became humble and stationary.

Despite our best efforts at survival from the land, our economic situation didn't improve. "When a new minister is elected to a village, he does not receive salary immediately," I wrote home. "We shall probably receive no salary for the month of April, as payment must date from the first of a month, and we began work on the sixth." The government continued to pay both ministers and teachers on an irregular schedule.

As Unitarian parishes went, Meszko was not considered a good village financially. After only a few months, our economic situation became acute. We could not have survived, much less set up the rudiments of a home, without generous supplements from my family and friends, especially Aunt Isabel and Uncle Mellen, who sent at least $10 every month.

We debated about how to use Isabel's money in a way that would be the most appropriate reminder of her, and decided on peasant kitchen furniture made to old Szekler designs. We painted the furniture in lovely Magyar flowers and put the date (1930) on them, in true peasant fashion. "Isabo's kitchen" made a big difference to me, as we had been more or less camping there.

Though pleasant enough in appearance, our house was a leaky old ark, with rough, splintery board floors difficult to keep clean. None of the rooms except the kitchen got sunlight, which was serious from the point of Feri's vulnerability to tuberculosis and my propensity for colds. During our first summer in the village, we spent most of our days on the porch and out of doors. When we felt the congregation had recovered from the shock of the cement floor in the barn, we planned to ask for some windows in the southwest side of the house.

Life became more adventurous when sturdy Agnes came into our lives. The spring in the center of the village was partly covered by an uptilted slab of rock. One day there, my eye caught sight of an almost invisible figure bending beside it, battering her bucket and splashing herself in the effort to get the water. As we drew near, I had an impression of a stocky girl, dwarf-like, hair drawn skin-tight, a creature made by and for rough work. Then she threw up her head. Her eyes, as they stared at us with surprise, were arrestingly beautiful. They were matched by her pleasantly resonant voice, "Yoy! You must be the new *Tiszteletes Ur*! My God, look out!"

Galloping down on us were about eight enormous white oxen, intent only on the water. Their long horns sticking out at least two feet on each side of their heads made a dancing threat of spears. Two of the great beasts began a sparring match beside us, cavorting around each other, bracing foreheads in a relentless pushing contest backed by the strength of their massive shoulders. They turned quickly aside for a clash of horns. I ducked behind a moss-covered watering trough while Feri futilely flourished his arms. The oxen's owners, finally catching up with them, could only shout insults to the oxen's mothers.

The young girl placed her water bucket carefully on the stone slab. Watching her chance, she stepped in between the oxen, adroitly seizing a long horn, and bore down heavily with all her weight. The great creature was swung away against his will, and the owners gained courage to take over.

"I'm Agnes," she said, as we continued our introductions.

When we were married, our most beautiful present arrived in Agnes's arms, a large white hen with a red rose tucked under each wing. "She'll lay you an egg every day," Agnes beamed. Because eggs were scarce, the hen was a valuable gift.

Another scarce item in the village was firewood. Any vestiges of bushes and trees had long disappeared from the windswept plateau above, and the willows near the river were kept sparse by the villagers' basket- and fence-weaving. A couple of days away by wagon was a forest from which the church was allowed to take a limited supply of firewood for the minister. A donation lay in our courtyard, a bristling pile of uncut green trees. How to cope with it? How to kindle the few damp boughs I managed to fit into our stove? Sometimes Feri was around when I needed him, but often not. Besides, we both had been ill and needed to refrain from heavy labor.

Who should come along one day to save us again but Agnes! Swinging an axe like a man, she soon had a supply of logs for me. As for kindling, she said, "Look, Tiszteletes Asszony, there's that old pigsty. It's falling down. No Pap has kept pigs for ages, and I don't guess you're going to." Agnes began to pluck off the dangling boards of the pigsty. "And here's this broken hen house door," she continued, "and this bit of fence." Unscrupulously, she showed me how to turn wreckage into good use.

The unfamiliar cycle of food growing, gathering, preserving, and cooking was my domain. Feri took care of his peasant responsibilities by turning over our acres of grain-growing land to a man for a half share of the crop. The vegetable-growing acres remained my problem.

An American cookbook Aunt Isabel sent me proved useless. Half the items in it were unobtainable, and the measurements were in American pounds instead of Hungarian kilos. I began to learn the routines from my neighbors and Agnes: bread and milk or chicory-stretched coffee for breakfast. For lunch, bread and soup or the universal *lashka*—homemade noodles rolled so thin as to cover the table like a cloth, and cut with finesse into an infinite variety of shapes, depending on whether it was to be served with cheese, poppy seeds, meat, or ground walnuts. For supper, always polizska. The cornmeal wasn't ground American style, but into a fine flour, then dropped as an unbroken mountain into a large kettle of boiling water, where it sat for half an hour. Just before serving, the watery meal was beaten with a thin pole into a very thick paste then dumped on a board and cooled until it could be sliced neatly with a string. Polizska was eaten with milk or stacked with alternating layers of cheese.

Soups—caraway, bean, apple, tomato, potato, onion, or parsnip—were thickened with flour browned darkly in lard, and glorified with noodles. Noodle cutting had many variations, from the long ribbons and strings to tiny diamond shapes called "wheat-seed," or thumb-sized rolls known as "angel's penis." Meat was a luxury. Meszko bread was round and gargantuan, loaves two feet in diameter. The week's baking for a family was four to ten loaves at a time, thrust on a wooden snow shovel into an outdoor clay oven that resembled an igloo.

Agnes helped me bargain with a Gypsy for a glorious, huge copper kettle to make cheese. It shone like the sun. She brought my first batch of sheep's milk, then advised me to get my own sheep, since most families in Meszko produced only for themselves. I had visions of a flock of lambs capering in our courtyard. But the village shepherd, a realistic and practical fellow, got hold of me. "The rams of our village flock are worn out. Won't you replace them? Three rams equal six sheep, as far as your share of milk from the herd goes," he reasoned. Persuaded, I took ten precious dollars—gift of Aunt Isabel—and set forth with Agnes to the animal fair. We chose three shaggy, dirty, curly-horned *berbecs* who were soon posted to the hilltop to do their duty by the ewes.

Every fifteen days, it was my turn to climb the hill and scan the horizon for the flock. The shepherd was a Romanian, who would come to visit me and the other owners of the flock during the winter to collect his pay in bread and bacon. Taking my wooden tub between his knees, he would squat beside a narrow gap in his movable willow fences, invite the sheep to file through, and extract a few squirts from each. I once tried to limit the bacteria count in the milk by taking a jug of water and a towel to the shepherd. He gave me a look as if I were crazy, then used my clean milk tub as his washbasin.

In my enthusiasm for living as a villager, I often overstepped the bounds. Agnes became my mentor in matters of decorum, gently telling me that the Tiszteletes Asszony could not go barefoot, even in her own house and garden. Nor must the Tiszteletes Asszony lose caste by wearing homespun cloth or rinsing clothes in the river or taking her own wheat to the mill.

Through Agnes, I became aware of a series of class attitudes based upon the amount of land a family owned, whether their wagon was pulled by a horse or a cow, if they had a wagon at all, or if their milk came from cows, buffalo, or goats. The village expected me to reflect these attitudes, but I could not. Once while weeding close to a fence I overheard Agnes on the other side discussing me with wondering approval. "She treats everybody alike," she exclaimed.

Preserving for the winter got me down. All summer I had to pick in small lots from the garden as things ripened, tie the canning jars with wet parchment paper stretched tight as a drum, tote heavy basketfuls to whatever house in the village happened to be baking, and shove them onto the hot bricks for sterilizing.

"I'm just no good as a peasant. I need help all the time!" I finally admitted to Feri. Though it would take a third of his salary to pay a girl, in the end I knew it would be worth it. But whom could we get? "I'd like to have Agnes," I ventured.

"I doubt if she'd come," Feri responded, "since she's the mainstay of her family. Besides, she's pretty *durva* (rough)."

"I don't care! I like her voice. She knows the ropes, and I like the way she laughs," I insisted. To the surprise of the village, her family, and myself, Agnes agreed to work for us. Although hired girls slept in the kitchen, usually on top of the table, which extended into a bed, we provided Agnes with a tiny room off the kitchen. Unlike other "gentlewomen," I wore no enormous keys around my waist to unlock every closet, drawer, or cupboard, or to hand out a sugar lump or dishrag to a servant. But Agnes had her own ideas about her place in the household. She came to me with her plate to have me dole out her food, then squatted on the doorsill to eat.

As we encouraged her to feel at home, Agnes began to assume her true shape. She soon spirited Feri's Hungarian translations of Bernard Shaw and Dostoyevsky into her room. "I know I am only a *paraszt* (a derogatory word for "peasant")," she would begin, then with more and more frequent bursts of assertion, "but this is what I think ..."

One day after church she remarked, "Your husband always says something you can think about. Not just 'Our God, our God,' like other ministers. You know, village folk are stupid. They do and say things over and over in the same old way." With a conspiratorial chuckle, Agnes continued, "I served a family in a city once. I used to steal their books, and I came to understand many things. When I dusted their writing desk, sometimes I read their letters, too. They started right out with something the person thought!" adding with a triumphant nod, "Something he thought of by himself."

The Meszko hilltop swept gently and endlessly upward to the sky. Agnes took me to hoe corn on "scoundrel's height."

"How come people ever chose to live on such a rocky hillside, without decent water?" I asked.

Dropping her hoe, Agnes drew an arm across her sweaty forehead. "Water, that's a good thought. Come, I'll show you where they say we used to live." She took me to the very edge of the horizon. The ploughed earth ended in a downward sweep of luxuriant grass growing among giant boulders. At the bottom, the noisy Aranyos river disappeared into the steep gorge. It was a precipitous and breathtaking scene. Fern-covered walls of rock rose in pinnacles and turrets.

Agnes made her way carefully to a spring of cold, pure water. "The Tartar invaders of the thirteenth century, they say, drove our ancestors away from here," she said solemnly, staring at the awesome Torda Gorge. "They say that all this was once just like the plain behind us, but when Szent Laszlo was fleeing before the barbaric Cumans, the earth cracked open suddenly to protect him."

What Agnes failed to teach me, Jula Neni filled in. With water so scarce, my garden was often a heartbreak. When there was no rain, Jula Neni and I doled out what we could carry to a few favorite plants. Beans were always a comfort; they survived anything and Jula Neni brought me endless varieties. The ones she assured me were "walking beans" would often as not climb to the heavens. Jula Neni would appear, flourishing a balloon-like squash. "You're not to eat this," she would announce. "It's for the seeds."

Then followed a cross-examination in which I would rate zero. "Did you save some of your *dobletsz*, *petrezselyem* (parsley), and *murak* for seed?"

"No, Jula Neni, we ate them all up."

"Did you bring in the roots of the white dahlia I gave you so they wouldn't freeze?"

"No, Jula Neni."

Learning was a two-way process, however. Ideas slipped out of our government bulletins and the *Britannicas* into the fields of Meszko, as well as the introduction of asparagus and rhubarb, rust-resistant grains and chemical fertilizer. A fruit-spraying apparatus we demonstrated soon became village property.

Jula Neni was a mixture of bitterness and joy—bitterness for being married to a limping, aged husband, and joy in the child of that marriage. Despite extreme poverty, her Ilonka was as sturdy and debonair as any well-cared-for American child. If Ilonka had been away at school for the morning, Jula Neni would gather her into a passionate embrace, crying, "My heart, my star!"

"They say I am foolish about her, Tiszteletes Asszony. I've never allowed her to carry water pails uphill, or heavy baskets to Torda. They say I'll make her lazy. But she'll have time to find out there's enough work to keep anybody from being lazy!"

The affection Feri and I felt for this mother and daughter and whatever help we were able to be to them were more than returned. If Jula Neni came to me with an aching tooth (which I treated as best I could, the only alternative being a pair of pliers), she was always turning up to take hoe or broom out of my hands. When Feri took little Ilonka to the doctor in Torda because of a danger of blood poisoning, we were repaid many times over with strawberries, green peas, and walnuts.

Suffering moved Jula Neni to tears. Unabashed, she would blot them with her apron or let them roll quietly down her brown cheeks, as when she had to sell their miserable little horse and watched the Gypsy buyers whipping him about the marketplace, or when the tax collector carried away the pillows off their beds, or when she thought I was homesick, or Feri ill.

Jula Neni was glad of any excuse to tell stories of her childhood. "My father was a builder and I was just like him, always whittling and carving away at scraps of wood.

"'Jula, if only you'd been born a son,' he'd say sadly.

"I could handle a saw almost as well as a man, and when I was only ten, I often helped him saw his big timbers. My eye was straighter than his, and once when we were chalking a new piece, I dared to correct him. He struck me such a blow I staggered and fell, yet before he could stop me I rushed into the house for a measuring stick and proved myself. From then on, my father respected me as if I had been born his son. Now don't think it isn't good for the young to be afraid of their parents. When I began to go out with boys, Father took me by the shoulders and said, 'My child, if ever you bring disgrace on the family I'll beat you till your eyes fly up to the stars!'

"A neighbor brought us a letter from a brother who had gone to America and wanted a Magyar wife sent over to him. I was ready for anything, to get away. Mother made me two new dresses for America, and I was all packed up, ready for the train, when she cried: 'Yoy! What am I doing, letting my girl go so far? She may drown in the ocean or may never come back!' I don't want to speak against the dead, God rest them, but a mother can ruin a child's life. A few years ago that man came back from America, and what wonderful things he brought! He was able to buy a house, and was a good man, too.

"Ilonka, go and fetch my shawl," she cried suddenly. When the child was out of hearing, Jula Neni continued her tale. "It was Mother who insisted that I marry Laci. He was twenty-five years older than I, and when we went shopping for the wedding I made him wait outside the stores so people wouldn't guess he was the bridegroom. That old carcass! What haven't we suffered together! He went to war and I resolved that when he came back, I'd quit. But while he was away Ilonka came.

"And yet, two people get along. I'll never forget the first dance after we were married. I asked him, 'Can you dance?'

"'No,' said he, but he went right on polishing up his boots, and when we got to the dance, the old liar, how he whirled me around! After that we went to all the dances. If it hadn't been for that and all the songs I know, I'd have gone mad, married to him here in Meszko.

"Yoy! The time he broke both his legs in the forest and I dragged him home on my back! For two months he lay in bed and I couldn't get out to the fields. A neighbor asked why didn't I tie a rope to the rafter above his bed so he could pull himself up and turn himself over with it. I did, and I felt so free, going away for the first time in days to hoe the corn.

"But while I was out in the field the thought suddenly struck me, 'What if the Old One uses that rope to hang himself?' I flew home, afraid to death of what I might see when I got there. I found him fast asleep, but I tell you I cut the rope down in a hurry and didn't leave him again."

By the end of our first summer in the village, confidence in our health had been restored. When Feri returned from leading an all-Transylvanian conference for young people, we visited a tuberculosis specialist. He said Feri's recovery was extraordinarily good and that I was all right too; in fact, able to bear a child. But he noted a tiny spot on my lung. Feri said the spot was in glands around my heart that usually get calcified in everybody. I wondered how the doctor could say so readily that I could bear a child if my lungs were not completely cleared up?

The Children of Meszko

In a village home I discovered an old cradle in the corner. As I examined its worn carving, I rocked it. "Don't do that!" cried several women, almost in one voice. "Don't you know that if a newly married woman rocks a cradle, her firstborn will die?"

Childbirth in Meszko was not an occasion for rejoicing. The first five babies born in the village after we came did not live. All were premature. Peasant babies arrived in every way unprepared for. Green as I was, I soon rushed to and fro to gather the wherewithal to care for them, taking the situation much more to heart than the mothers.

The first baby was born in a kitchen so barren that I could not find a pot suitable to boil water in. The tiny baby was unable to nurse. I kept coming to feed it a bottle because I suspected that Erzsi, its mother, wouldn't bother. She was afraid of her husband, who doubted that the child was his. Both seemed relieved when it died. When they later had a son, a little blue-eyed replica of his father, Erzsi was restored to her husband's rough graces.

Another villager, Anna, was dismayed to find that she had given birth to twins. "Yoy! I was afraid of that. But the little boy is weak; the good God probably won't let him live," she said. Anna seemed relieved when my efforts to save the infant failed, "because I can go out to the fields with a baby in one hand and my tools in the other. But with *two* babies!"

I urged another mother to let me drive her baby to the doctor in Torda. "If the good God wants him to die, he'll die anyway. Why take him to a doctor?" she asked with a shrug.

I asked Jula Neni, "When a baby is dangerously ill, would they take him to the doctor or the Pap?"

"Pap, of course," she replied immediately.

I witnessed a number of hasty christenings for fear that the baby, centered on a huge lace-trimmed pillow, would die without a name. Peasant births became even more hazardous under Romanian rule. A law that all midwife training had to be conducted in Romanian effectively barred most Hungarian midwives, so many villages were without trained assistance.

In Meszko, the *Baba* (midwife) was an elderly Romanian woman with no other qualification other than experience. She was kindly but superstitious and without knowledge of the importance of sterilized procedures. Soon the Baba was rivaled by the new Gypsy blacksmith's wife, armed with a desperate need of money and her hard, sparkling self-assurance. Because of my insistence on cleanliness in such matters, I came to be called upon along with these two. I soon learned local traditions or superstitions, such as not sitting on a new mother's bed for fear the milk would be transferred from her breasts to mine, and always bathing the newborn with a brand new cake of soap.

One day I visited a neighbor who, assisted by the Baba and a neighbor, had just given birth to her tenth child. She was in great pain, looking as if life had been drained out of her. The birth had taken place in her home, an old thatched house with a dirt floor and the barest of furniture. The four smallest children were huddled together like a litter of piglets. All were without proper food and clothing. I couldn't imagine where they slept. The woman's husband was rough and surly.

"Whatever one may think of artificial birth control, it's a necessity in a case like this," I wrote to Aunt Isabel. "I foresee myself as a dispenser of it in the village as soon as I learn where and how it may be obtained."

The next day, the tiny newborn was brought to our house to be christened. "They are afraid it won't live," I wrote home, "and I could not be very sorry if it did not, for the mother's sake. If only one had a little means to do certain simple, necessary things!"

I pitted the full strength of my persuasion against the swaddling of babies. Even in midsummer, the tiny creatures would be bound round and round, legs stiff, arms to the sides until they looked almost like clothespins. Even the head was bound as far down as the eyes, only the wizened face visible. The villagers believed that if an infant's legs weren't held forcibly straight for at least a month, they would be bent throughout life.

I preached prenatal and infant care, my bible being the US government bulletins. I longed for a microscope. The villagers thought that what could not be seen did not exist, and that bacteria was a curious American superstition. (When I returned to America, I found that at least in one respect the peasant women of Meszko were wiser than I. Their "primitive" custom of feeding their babies when they cry, rather than according to a schedule, was becoming gradually accepted by child care authorities back home.)

My experiences in the village with new life and death encouraged me to reflect on what it would be like to have a child. I truly wanted one, and felt healthy enough to become pregnant. In late fall of 1930, I was indeed with child. Delighted, I promptly named it "O" (Hungarian for "it" and pronounced *eu*). Soon I began calling it Little Person. Pregnancy brought me much inner peace and tranquility as well as increased domesticity. I discovered new pleasure in just putting clean cases on the pillows.

One day as I was putting my empty spools on a string for the baby in the thatched house across the street, it occurred to me that I should be saving such things now for our own child. Nevertheless, I didn't believe that I would ever completely feel like a mother. I could more easily think of Little Person as a future playmate or contemporary.

At the time, I was reading H. G. Wells's *Love and Mr. Lewisham*. In that story, a young husband struggles with having to sacrifice a career to the economic necessities of his marriage, and his social and professional interests to the more limited views of his uneducated wife. Then a child is on the way, providing a resolution: "Come to think, it is all the Child. The future is the Child. The Future. What are we—any of us—but servants or traitors to that? . . . Career? In itself it is a career—the most important career in the world."

"I cannot quite share this view," I wrote Aunt Isabel. "My greatest hope is that the Little Person may in its own way find life as absorbing as I do, and more fully so. But I would never want to feel that the child *is* my life or my career, though it is an essential part of it. I always used to feel such tremendous sadness and protest at the thought that Mother lived mainly for me, because I so much wanted Life, in itself, to be the greatest good for her. This can be so, I believe, even if one is as cruelly disabled as she was."

Only two weeks later, in early December, I had to write: "Bogy, what wouldn't I give not to have to write this letter. My little baby has gone. Due to infection of a severe influenza, the doctor said. I was in the hospital in Torda for ten days. The course of the whole affair was 'normal,' they say. An x-ray of my chest shows that I have come through without any lighting up of the old trouble. I am at home now, in Meszko, directing the household from bed, where I shall stay until I am through coughing. It's a horrid cough . . . like whooping cough . . . so deep I almost vomit.

"For several days I had felt restive and ill at ease. One night I woke up at midnight and half-asleep, proposed to Feri that I return to America so the little one might be born in greater security. Then came a cold, temperature and an all-over achiness so suggestive of influenza that I went to bed. After twenty-four hours the acute symptoms disappeared and I had a tremendous desire to work.

"Next morning at eleven o'clock the bleeding began. For a moment I was terrified at the thought that it might mean the loss of the baby. . . . So I lay down again, called Rozsie, told her to hitch up Jancsi and go at once to Torda to meet Feri's two o'clock bus from Kolozsvár. He must get word to Dr. Kovacs.

"Then began the most terrible coughing I had ever experienced. For the next eight hours, as I lay there waiting, I waged an agonizing battle with that wrenching cough. Whenever I coughed a rush of blood came, and I would fear that this particular cough or the next might be the one to break the little baby's final hold on life. Then pains began . . . so like what I had heard of birth pains, that whatever hope I had for the little one became more and more desperate.

"Turning again and again to the booklet, I found an alarming sentence which you had underlined: 'a neglected miscarriage may mean a total loss of health.' At three in the afternoon, Uci, a sixteen-year-old village girl, came to see me. I sent her immediately to call Kovacs, the schoolteacher. . . . After I described precisely my need, he promptly disappeared and discovered a wagon just setting forth for Torda. He had my note saying that Feri must be sure to bring the doctor with him.

"At seven in the evening, Jancsi rolled in with Rozsie and Feri. . . . Dr. Kovacs was on her way in a closed car, in case I had to return with her to the hospital. Presently Dr. Kovacs arrived, a grotesque little figure, but comfortingly full of life and confidence. Her face immediately became sober when she saw the extent of the bleeding. After a quick examination she declared: 'No, there is nothing to be done; the uterus is already opened.' When Feri came in, Dr. Kovacs told him, then said briskly to me, 'Now! The thing for all of us to do now is to look after your health! You must get ready to come with me to the hospital. All the warm clothes you've got!'

"Roszie and Feri bundled me up and Dr. Kovacs gave me an injection of morphine to lessen the pain during the journey. The schoolteacher hitched up his two cows, and Rozsie made me a bed of straw in the bottom of the wagon. Soon I was trundling over the rocky, alabaster road through the village. The slow cart took the bumps more gently than an automobile could have.

"That night, I remember, was especially beautiful. As I looked straight up into a sky crowded with stars, I placed my precious babe among the farthest of them."

During the journey to the hospital, I remembered a sudden, overwhelming realization I had experienced shortly after hearing of my mother's death. "Perhaps all your fine and lovely qualities will not be lost," I had said to my mother's spirit. "Someday I shall have a child and you will be present in her or him." But I had the feeling that this child was especially Feri's. I imagined that he had given his very best to this first child.

When Feri and I walked about the village, small children stared from a safe distance or ran shrieking. Mothers were accustomed to saying, "Be good or the Pap will cut out your tongue."

"*Nem szabad*! (Not allowed!)" was always heard when children were around. They soon discovered that Feri was not that kind of Pap. Not so with the Tanito. Like most Hungarian teachers, Kovacs was a martinet, a role strengthened by nerve-wracking Romanian requirements. Not only did the schoolchildren have to learn Romanian, they had to carry on most of their work in the new, alien tongue.

The Hungarian school was a bleak room with long, high planks for desks and lower ones for seats. The Tanito had a real desk mounted on a platform. On his desk lay a willow switch. As Feri and I came in on our first visit, forty-odd youngsters hopped to their feet, shouting in unison, "God brought you!" Kovacs, sandy haired, with high cheekbones and slightly oblique eyes, bowed stiffly and commanded the children to sit. The tone of the room was gray, I decided, because of a series of lurid pictures of fierce-eyed, mustachioed warriors mowing down the enemy; in some cases, ancestors of these children. The frieze had been supplied by the state.

"Yes," said the Tanito, following our glance, "the Romanians are just waiting for an excuse to take over our school."

"But didn't I just hear you doing geography in Hungarian?" Feri teased.

"Of course," replied Kovacs, his inscrutable mask breaking into a grin as he told how lucky he had been. "Whenever a Romanian inspector drops in, he finds a perfect Romanian program in full swing. We have a little system. At the first school up the valley, a little boy goes to the outhouse, then scoots across the fields to warn the next school, which warns the next, and so on."

The Tanito wheeled suddenly. A rogue-faced little girl had been whispering to her neighbor. "Come here!" roared Kovacs, boxing her ears hard. Pointing her to a crack in the wall, he told the child to lean forward and place her nose against it and stand on one leg for half an hour.

Having one's picture taken was a rare and solemn occasion for the Hungarian Unitarian school children. Standing in the back is their teacher Kovacs Janos.

"Let's go," I whispered to Feri. My educational bias was causing me pain, and I could do nothing about it. Another day, I watched the schoolchildren being examined by the Romanian supervisor. The youngsters were scared to death, rattling off like machines about things that had no meaning to them. Kovacs was nervous, ready to bite the children's heads off if they made mistakes. His job depended upon their showing. If little Kato slipped up on the provinces of Greater Romania, she got five lashes with the switch on her outstretched palm.

Even though the cultural autonomy of the Hungarian schools was supposedly guaranteed, it was being taken away on any pretext. To Isabel I wrote, "It is terrible . . . people everywhere become dead machines. How paradoxical that in the schools there is no time for real education, to develop intelligent thinking men and women with resources to meet the problems here."

Sadly, the church was part of the problem. "I am reminded again and again by Unitarianism here of its pre-Unitarian origins," I wrote to Dr. Earl Wilbur. "As the time of confirmation draws near, fourteen year olds must memorize from a book of catechism the answers to one hundred fifty questions. Here's a sample: 'What is the greatest proof of the fatherly love of God?' Answer: 'That in the beginning He placed the first couple in the paradise of Eden.' These answers they must recite before the assembled congregation."

Despite the harsh routines, many youngsters possessed traits prized by progressive schools, such as practical initiative and skilled use of their hands. By the age of six, they could commandeer the family oxen, harvest potatoes, and watch their parents do things like spinning, weaving, carving an ox yoke, constructing a wagon wheel, and helping a calf to be born.

"Has anybody shoveled your manure today?" seven-year-old Pista would shout manfully. Lena, a little Romanian girl of cork-like buoyancy and unfailing grin, would join in wiping dishes or picking berries. If there was nothing else to do, she would seize a broom and stir dust up from the cracks in our kitchen floor.

During our first days in Meszko, the children's genuine appreciation of the few events we arranged for them surprised and encouraged us. At the start of the three-day Easter festival, we gave an evening program. Feri spoke about China and I taught two girls to work my Chinese shadow puppets in the play that he and I had written for them. We held open house for young people one afternoon, and then one for children the next—about a hundred people on each occasion. The children came hesitatingly at first. They were afraid that we would be like the previous minister, who used to cuff them.

As the fun increased, black-kerchiefed, black-shawled mothers peeped shyly over the fence. Soon there was an audience of about thirty parents: fathers in rough, gray, homespun woolen trousers; mothers with babies in their arms, enjoying the games as much as the children. We taught them croquet, volleyball, and other games. Our croquet set was courtesy of a check from American friends. The Romanian children could not resist the crack of the croquet balls and came at first when they were sure of having the courtyard to themselves.

When I told the children they could use our outdoor kitchen for one of our dreams—a children's house—they worked with whirlwind enthusiasm. Twenty girls mixed clay and straw to patch the crumbling walls. They renewed the floor with a time-honored mixture of clay and horse manure, which their bare feet danced to proper consistency. In a few hours it was hard, odorless, and cleanly sanded. They whitewashed the walls and plastered them with pictures snipped from my American magazines: Henry Ford was sandwiched between a Chinese actor and a Brazilian monkey, and society belles vied with tropical fish. Aunt Isabel sent fifty boxes of crayons, and I donated the gay and artistic picture books I had picked up in Moscow on my journey here. The Meszko carpenters called a *kalaka* (voluntary gathering) and worked for a day on tables and benches.

Our courtyard swarmed with children sprawling on the steps with Russian picture books; young people standing against the porch railing, deep in our *Britannicas*; ten youngsters around one table, busy with the crayons; sixteen at another, modeling for the first time with clay dug from the hillside.

Presently, what I hoped for happened: About seventy children crowded the place, a bedlam of happy chatter in both tongues. The Hungarian and Romanian mothers finally ventured in to try their hand at drawing and modeling. The walls of the Children's House became covered with drawings that showed a wonderful sense of design, color, and originality, the geometrical Romanian distinguishable from the freer Hungarian art.

In no time at all, ten to forty children were coming to the Children's House nearly every afternoon; on Sunday afternoons about eighty came. Even the sixteen year olds would leave their Sunday afternoon dance to come over for an hour of play.

One holiday afternoon, all the young people in the village descended upon me. I was alone and a little taken aback, as my Hungarian was far from perfect, but there was no difficulty. They were so interested in pictures of travel and adored my opera glasses! About twenty young men and women were quietly absorbed in our papers and magazines. They had literally nothing to read in their homes, and no public library. Even village ministers could afford but few books. The children were ravenous for books. In school each child had one book, a Hungarian-Romanian reader. Some of them planned a play to try to earn enough money to buy three or four good books. But what were three or four books among a village full of children of all ages?

One day no Romanian children came to the Children's House. Their teacher, finally aware of the unprecedented gatherings, had forbidden them. Next, the Romanian authorities announced, "The Hungarian school in Meszko is too small. If it is to continue, it must be torn down and enlarged." At first this puzzled us, as the Romanian school was even smaller, had more children, and its roof was threatening to fall in. Since the burden of replacing a separate Hungarian school would fall on the Hungarians in the village, the official tactic became clear. The message to the parents was: Build a new schoolhouse or send your children to the Romanian school.

With fatalism compounded by poverty, the Hungarians were inclined to do nothing. Feri took on the issue, tramping from one meeting and office to another, persuading and plowing through endless legal red tape. Finally, the result—a large, well-lit schoolhouse with pillars and beamed ceilings gaily carved and colored in Hungarian designs by local artisans. The school even had a workshop with a workbench, tools, a library, and a little co-op supply store run by the children themselves. The Romanian inspector grudgingly admitted that it was the best in the district.

Feri felt that the preservation of Hungarian culture, though important, was secondary to the need for critical intelligence and the will to live positively. Remembering that the first folk high schools of Denmark were held in the teacher's house, we used our living room for education, since the young men and women in Meszko had no place to call their own. In our community gatherings the young people read Hungarian poet Petofi Sandor and studied world history, with many lively discussions. Whenever a Transylvanian Pap joined a group, they usually fell silent while he sermonized. It shocked visiting ministers to find that this was no longer happening in Meszko, at least among the Unitarians.

"A folk school is the thing! More and more I'm convinced of it," I wrote to my Aunt Grace. "Here are one hundred twenty villages with young men and women as intelligent as anywhere else in the world. A folk school would be their starting point, with a good library, two or three teachers of imagination, and equipment for self-support: gardens, a shop, carpentry, weaving loom, perhaps a pottery kiln. Once their minds began to move they'd see the advantages of cooperative methods of agriculture, and these forlorn villages would begin to live again."

I selected a spot for the folk high school—the vineyard—six acres on a southward hilltop, with the most superb view of the countryside, the whole sweep of the river valley and the far-off russet mountains. It was to be a dream unrealized. But the young people of Meszko eventually rented a room in a peasant house for games of chess and ping pong, and spinning, reading, and singing.

On Sunday evenings we held folk school in the schoolhouse. Sometimes almost two hundred people came. Feri arranged the programs until the villagers became used to speaking. A man who was something of an outlaw from a neighboring village read his stories. A doctor came from Torda to speak on a much-needed aspect of health. Men who had been prisoners of war in Italy or Siberia told their experiences. Mazsi Bacsi, a wizened elf of a man, recollected old tales that otherwise would have died with him. Shy women like Jula Neni recited long poems. How they enjoyed it and how well they did! If older minds went blank, a youngster was usually ready with the cue. When I managed to learn Hungarian sufficiently to get beyond the stage of embarrassment, I gave weekly lectures to village women, usually on health and nutrition. The gatherings in the school were crowded as the church was not, because women unable to afford a store-bought black silk church dress were willing to come. The village was coming together.

I had almost forgotten about radio until Feri's brother gave us one. I was as incredulous as any villager to think that the silent air of our remote hillside had been buzzing with uncaught music, wild golden bees of sound, silently in flight. When dance music from Vienna came through, my feet became delirious. Supper danced onto the table. Soon, voices came crowding in from Budapest, Rome, and Prague. My spell of loneliness was broken.

One evening, a throng of men and women gathered on our porch, stood on the steps and sat on benches in the courtyard, listening to their own Ernó Dohnanyi conduct the Budapest Symphony Orchestra. The next evening, several young alabaster miners listened for two hours to Tchaikovsky and Grand Opera from Naples. Before one meeting of our Agricultural Society, thirty men sat hunched and silent, attentively listening to old Magyar folk songs on our radio.

The villagers danced on Sunday afternoons in an open barn. Three Gypsies with violin, cello, and bass appeared from no one knew where. The importunate music would pile up to a climax and die on a note of despair, to pick up again in a haze of scintillating grace. It went on and on, far into the night. At those dances, wooden faces were lit up from within. Kovacs would seize Agnes and whirl dizzily, never losing their light precision of step; stamping, shouting, separating to snap their fingers and twirl alone for a moment, then uniting to spin with such speed that Agnes's skirt became a fan.

She would start to sing:

Round is the cabbage, crinkly its leaves,
Come to my arms, my sweetheart.

Kovacs or some other young man might carry on:

Do you see, my darling,
Do you see that distant mountain?

To which came the reply:

As long as I see that mountain,
As long as I see that mountain,
I will never be yours.
That mountain I'll carry away
  in the four corners of my handkerchief!
Then, only yours, only yours will I be,
  my sweet dove.

Working Together

Even though our house was drafty that fall and winter, the main room was cozy. I decorated it with our art collection from the Orient, one or two nice pieces of peasant embroidery, my Indian blanket, and the silver tea set from my Danish grandmother. On the doors I tacked pieces of printed Japanese cloth. We painted Feri's big church desk and the cupboard blue, and the porch table, kitchen table, shelves, waterstand, and washstand green. We tinted whitewash for the walls a pale buff yellow. For the sake of our health I painted the floor too, as the rough boards were unspeakably dusty.

I began to toy with the idea of returning to America to teach for a couple of years to get us out of debt, but Feri wouldn't hear of it. When I wasn't depressed over our home economy, I found myself reflecting on our interesting and difficult life. When I received my first letter addressed to Christine Balázs, it gave me a funny, inexplicable feeling. I didn't like having my own name taken away.

I wrote to Aunt Isabel, "Don't, please don't feel like weeping when you think of it. . . . Whatever my difficulties may be, they are always interesting, and are bound up with events and people near and far, in history and space.

"I am 'caught in a net,' as you say. It is an unfinished net, however, with many loose ends that one can pick up and work on, provided one is unconventional enough to discover them. . . . It's the world net, and you and Uncle Mellen are in it, too, and the Peninsula School, and American Unitarians and Danish Folk Schools, and Antioch, and Father and Mother and Helen and Dr. Sharman. My first loneliness is gone. You are all with me, and I am with you.

"As Feri and I see certain things gradually happening, we look at each other with amazement and delight, and can't help exclaiming, 'Isn't it just too lovely!' 'It' may best be summed up in the words of a villager who observed that since we had been here 'the village is coming together.' Things are only at their beginning, but such sound and hopeful beginnings.

"Three bells must ring in our little toy church before we go," I continued, "and the first is tolling now. As you know, I have always had some doubts about being attached to a church, as I am unable to comply with much of its forms with any sincerity and interest. But I feel that this little building of peasant design is ours. We can make what we will of it. It is the only meeting place these 350 Hungarians have, and there is nothing to prevent its becoming a center of happy, meaningful events."

Our church's crumbling wooden tower held strong, resonant old bells. While the bell of the Greek Orthodox church beat with the rapid excitement of a fire alarm, our bells tolled out slowly, as if symbolizing the Unitarian creed, "God is One! God is One!" Men of the parish, young and old, gathered outside the church after Sunday services to discuss Feri's ideas. Several were avowed enemies of the church, with good reason in light of ecclesiastical emptiness and corruption. We took it as a sign of their intelligence.

"Yesterday the little church was crowded," I wrote home. "Everyone I could see, except one or two habitually sleeping old men, was listening with an alert expression. About yesterday's sermon, people said that it was the best they had ever heard in Meszko."

As tokens of their friendship, some of the parish men brought us vegetable and flower plants, insisting on planting them in our garden themselves. The villagers' appreciation took the form of frequent gifts such as eggs, potatoes, garden seeds, strings of onions, bread, cake, lettuce, parsley, cheese, and flowers. One rainy day when the streets were literally rivers of mud, one darling seventy-four-year-old man brought me his son's boots for fear my feet would get cold.

"I can say with confidence that I'm well, good weight and color, a beautiful burnished brown from haymaking, gardening, and bathing in the Aranyos," I could at last write home. "I love doing honest-to-goodness work, to some extent. It brings me in contact with the people as nothing else, and takes me out into the fields, which now are unbelievably lovely . . . a hundred varieties of wildflowers.

"I have been furiously preserving fruit and vegetables for the cold winter to come. So far, about 150 quarts of beans, corn, tomatoes, plums, cherries, apricots and currants. I am also burying a lot of plums and green peppers in ashes, and shall be interested in the outcome of this method of preservation advised by a neighbor."

Throughout that autumn, Agnes helped me like a Trojan, tough in mind as well as body. "The people are bad," she cautioned. "You have to watch them all the time." Our corn—several wagonloads—was dumped into three golden hills in our courtyard. Two were for us, and one was for the family who had cultivated it. Depending on where we decided to start, every second or third pile in the series was ours. "Watch out," whispered Agnes. "They think you are going to start with that big pile, but see how the piles beyond peter out." Or "Don't take that big pile—he's put it on a rise in the ground."

Agnes could be shrewd on her own behalf as well. On a visit to her grandmother's house, I stood as she peered up at me with rheumy eyes from under the mountain of her hunched back, which Agnes said was injured when she fell from an apple tree and landed with tremendous force on her feet. All the seams in the old woman's skin were filled with dirt, like a cellar potato. She lived like such a potato in her dirt-floored house, almost barren of furniture. Here was a heap of carrots, there a mound of unhulled beans, in the corner a pile of cabbages.

I stooped to shout in her ear, "Have you any eggs for sale?"

"I ask your very great pardon, Tiszteletes Asszony, for having addressed you as 'thou.' I cannot see or hear. I thought it was just a village girl," she responded.

She set to work with a collector's concentration. Out of a battered kettle at the back of the stove, one egg. Out of a pottery jug under a chair, three. Unknotting an old towel, she produced four more. Then out to the barn to pry under a sitting hen, and back with another. As I was counting the lei into her trembling hand, a hen flew out from the middle of her unmade bed with a squawk and left yet another egg.

"How do you manage all by yourself, Mali Neni?" I asked.

"Like an old woman," she responded matter-of-factly. "Let me offer you an apple," she said, digging one out from under a heap of rags and vegetables on the floor. "And some grapes," she continued, as she reached for one of three shrivelled bunches hanging from a rafter. "Aren't you going to eat them now?" she asked with obvious disappointment. "Well then, here's another bunch for the Pap."

"Say," the grandmother said, "Agnes said she took my meat grinder to use for you, and it broke and she had to take it to Torda to be mended. That was long ago."

I was silent, not knowing what to say. I had my own meat grinder.

"Agnes told me she took it home to keep for you because your house is open and she was afraid it would be stolen from you," she went on. As I remained silent, Mali Neni, with sudden suspicion, came to her own conclusion. "The dirty pig!" she cried out. "Agnes took it, for fear her brother will get it if I die. She'll lay up for herself, never fear!" Her mind began to wander. "Tiszteletes Asszony, when I die I don't want to be buried in one of those dresses they make for coffins. You know, which have just a front. Wouldn't I be embarrassed after I'm resurrected to walk down the road in Heaven in a dress without a back to it?"

That winter, Agnes was frequently depressed. I couldn't wonder, as she told me more and more about her family. Her father was one of the rough men of the village. He bullied her sickly mother and snatched whatever advantage he could from their many children. Agnes had been the buffer. "Children, always more children!" she said. "And Father never caring whether we were clothed or whether any of us had any peace in our soul. When Pali raised the baby pig Grandmother gave him to buy a winter suit for himself, Father took the money. And you know Samu, who is not right in his head? That's because Father hit him for not coming right away."

Agnes saw to it that her four brothers, one by one, were apprenticed in town. Only a young girl herself, she chose their trades, drove the terms with their masters, walked to Torda with their clean shirts, and battled with her father for their pocket money.

"Have you ever planned anything for yourself, Agnes?" I asked.

"Yoy," she responded, "I've wanted to get away from home, away from my father. There have been men willing to marry me even without any dowry, but every time—I don't know why it is—I go with a man, deep down there is always the panic that he may be *paraszt* (brutal), and I think: Yoy! What an escape."

"They say peasant life is simple," I remarked to Feri, "but I don't find it so."

To Aunt Isabel I wrote, "There is a government tax on sugar and many other things. Matches are frightfully expensive. The taxing policy of this government is abominable. For instance, the young people of the village are rehearsing plays. Feri has just been to Torda to go through all the red tape necessary for their public performance. He must write a petition to present the plays, for which there is a tax. When he receives the permission, there is another tax. If these young people clear 600 or 700 lei in admission fees, 400 must go for taxes!

"I just learned something shocking. The church retains every month one percent of each minister's salary. In this way it is able to pay the monthly *bribe* to the government, which is necessary to receive the salary at all! Imagine, the church bribes the state to pay its legitimate support. I almost feel that if the church must bribe a corrupt government for the maintenance of its organization, it would be better for it to refuse state aid, even to disband rather than suffer such humiliation and degradation of principle. If state-paid churches cease, need religion cease? Religious bodies in America are an answer. Payment of ministers would certainly cease here if the entire payment depended on the people.

"But the church situation here is complicated by national loyalties. Withdrawal of state aid from minority church schools would probably mean their closing, and the commitment of Hungarian children to Romanian schools is difficult to judge. One of the large Unitarian high schools here may be forced to close for lack of support from Unitarians themselves."

More than once we had to report to officials in Torda. The Secret Police always wanted to know the whole story of my intentions and purposes in staying in Romania. The long arm of the government even reached to the animals. One day we learned that our Jancsi and other horses must go to the village of Szan Mihaly to be conscripted in case of war. Happily, Jancsi was rejected because he hadn't shed his baby teeth. I felt like trying to fasten them in with sealing wax, in anticipation of the next year's conscription day! Then we heard that Donkee would also have to undergo conscription. Having witnessed a wagonload of nine or ten soldiers urging along one gasping, perspiring small horse, I felt like shouting, "I didn't raise my donkey to be a soldier!"

Not long after we purchased Jancsi, we hitched him to our wagon and set out for tea at one of the most elegant homes in Torda, dressed in our finest. Road repairing forced us to make a detour through foot-deep mud. Across our way lay a small ditch, but we decided we could make it if we took it very slowly. One moment we were sitting comfortably on the wagon seat, Isabel's green steamer rug under us, and my Indian blanket over us. The next moment I was stretched out on my stomach in the mud, wrapped in the steamer rug as neatly as in a cocoon.

I sat up and looked toward the wagon for Feri. Jancsi pulled steadily onward, unaware of any disaster, Feri nowhere in sight. I discovered him sprawled in the mud at my side, likewise wrapped in the Indian blanket! Our immediate reaction was shouts of laughter. We corralled Jancsi, and shortly presented ourselves at the tea party, immaculate but for muddy shoes and trouser legs.

After my fateful bout with influenza that resulted in the miscarriage, I had a relapse of the flu. Dr. Kovacs asked that I come to Torda for an examination. On a clear January morning we drove over dazzling snowfields. To our great relief, Dr. Kovacs pronounced everything in order.

After the doctor's visit we returned to our wagon, where Jancsi was placidly waiting and eating hay. I climbed up as usual, while Feri began to put the bit into Jancsi's mouth. Suddenly our angelic horse went into a fit of rage, perhaps because his hay-munching had been interrupted. He plunged forward, with Feri struggling to hold him. Turning from arranging the rugs to see Feri being dragged along the street, I shouted to him to let go, for fear he'd strain his chest. As I careened away on the wagon, my last glimpse was of Feri lying in the street.

Thus began the wildest ride of my life. Three men ran out at different times from the sidewalk to try to seize the bridle, whereupon Jancsi would veer sidewise with such violence that I was in danger of being overturned. After that, I frantically waved away other helpful pedestrians. I hadn't seen that the bit was not in Jancsi's mouth. My one thought was to untie the reins while keeping my balance.

Presently, instead of staying on the straight road, Jancsi took it into his head to try a corner. I was fascinated: Would we or would we not upset? We all but did and then went racing merrily on. I had freed the reins and was pulling mightily, but to no effect. Then, when I began calling and whistling to Jancsi, he pricked up his ears, slackened his mad pace, and came to a dead stop. A soldier ran out and gave Jancsi the bit, while I petted and soothed him.

When Feri came panting along we shouted in one breath, "Are you all right?" It was only then that he noticed his left hand was badly swollen and discolored. As we drove back to Dr. Kovacs to get it examined, a man stepped out from the sidewalk to present us with Feri's hat. Farther along, another stood waiting with the muddy blanket, and beyond him, a boy with a muddier pillow.

"Broken bone" was Dr. Kovacs's opinion of the hand. We drove to another part of town to a doctor whose x-ray equipment showed a neat break. Then to the hospital, where Feri stretched out on the very table where I had lain a short time before with the miscarriage.

It was dark when we set out for home with Feri's arm in plaster of paris. I drove once-more-angelic Jancsi. Amazingly, I didn't feel tired. But the next day brought me fever, chills, and a fierce head cold. Although I was soon better, recovering from the combination of miscarriage, flu, and a cold was slow. Trying to build up lost pounds and strength, I found it hard to strike the right balance between work and rest. I wrote to Aunt Isabel, "This is a cold old house, and I've just discovered why. Most houses here, if they have no cellar under them, at least have a deep solid bank of sand under the floor, but this one has neither cellar nor sand. We found a crack all around the base of the wall, through which blew a continuous draft strong enough to flutter a piece of paper! This we plugged with lime; nevertheless, my legs are cold as I sit in a chair.

"Our precious little baby. I was trying my best to take care, but conditions were too much for us. Oh, I worshiped that baby. If I ever have another child, I won't dare to love it so much. You know, legend repeats the theme in which God or the fairies take away the child because its mother loves it too much. I understand the source of such tales in human feeling."

Feri and I believed that human cooperation is as natural as competition. We found confirmation in the *Kopta*, Meszko's community garden. The path to the Kopta followed the caprice of the river, past an old mill with a wooden waterwheel and stone grinders, through a cool thicket and out to a bay with a vista of rugged blue mountains.

In the spring, a dozen teams of snowy oxen could be seen ploughing in the Kopta at the same time. Men, women, and children shouted and urged their long-horned oxen, black buffalo, and horses to turn up fresh black soil with their plows. In the summer it was a social place, with entire families weeding, gossiping, and singing, their water bottles and babies parked in the shade.

Years before, the village of Sinfalva, just across the river, laid claim to this beautiful spot. There was a pitched battle. When one peaceloving Meszko man saw that many men were getting hurt, he ran for his gun. He shot it into the air, so frightening the invaders that several of them nearly drowned in their effort to escape.

By the time Feri and I arrived in Meszko, the Kopta belonged to the church. Feri thought it exemplified the ideal in landholding: community ownership with temporary use by families according to need. When he delved into ancient records he found that the arrangement had not been prompted by idealism. On the contrary, one man had decided to grow cabbages in undeveloped wilderness. His neighbors could not bear to see such privilege. A minister had the foresight to prevent future division and sale, and, after a struggle, succeeded in guaranteeing the Kopta to the community for all time.

Meszko was a forlorn, primitive village with a difficult history. There were many other villages like it. What could be done to persuade groups of villages to work cooperatively? What ideas might help lift them out of poverty? It seemed reasonable to us that a group of villages could afford to pay a doctor and an agricultural expert and to form agricultural cooperatives.

Our first effort at economic uplift for the village centered on its scraggly poultry population. We started by introducing White Leghorns into our courtyard. Their classic purity and red combs suggestive of Greek helmets led us to name them after Greek gods and goddesses. Then we added a few Rhode Island Reds, who became the gods of Norse mythology. The two did not mix; the Greeks were nervous and quarrelsome, the Scandinavians placid and responsive. Because the villagers loved the Reds, Feri exchanged their brown eggs for ordinary eggs, which we ate.

Our next effort was with dairy. At dawn every day, Meszko women walked ten miles to Torda, each carrying a pottery jug of milk covered by a cabbage leaf. There they squatted in the dust of the market, with its uncertainty of prices and customers. Why not organize a milk cooperative? we thought. It might also be another way to bring Hungarians and Romanians together.

Our interest in a cooperative was partly selfish. Having become masters of much milk, Feri and I had to figure out what to do with it. When entering our kitchen, one was confronted with a panorama of milk in every kind of pan, jug, pot, kettle, basin, bowl, and cup. We hesitated about buying much equipment to handle our unexpected bounty, as we had only about $5. But finally it became necessary to buy a small milk separator for $18, which we purchased on time. It was the beginning of the milk and butter cooperative for the village.

Since nothing of the sort had been done there before, we couldn't expect the villagers to grasp the idea and make the initial investments. With a check from Unitarians in America, we purchased a wagon and donated our horse Jancsi to the cause. We rounded up regular customers in Torda and had a glass factory manufacture milk bottles, American style. Since there was no refrigeration, we built a low cement tank on the cool earth floor of our basement. Donkee did duty hauling water from the river to the tank. My job was to wash and sterilize the bottles. Using a long stick, I ducked them one by one into a kettle of boiling water and out again. Experience brought agility, and eventually the scalding drip didn't run up my arm. Capping the new-fangled bottles was a test of ingenuity that Feri met with a short piece of pipe sharpened at one end. Placing it on half a dozen squares of cardboard, he lambasted it with a wooden mallet. Then we immersed the full bottles up to their necks in the tank. We also had all the cows tested for tuberculosis.

In the evening, villagers came streaming in from all directions with their jugs of milk. At first Feri took their donations on faith, but he soon discovered that without exception their rough pottery containers were scanted. The shortage was made up by our extra contribution of milk, so Feri introduced exact measure.

I wrote to Aunt Isabel, "Feri and I have no doubt as to the importance of our job here. If education is to be real for these villagers it can only come through people who do not hold themselves aloof, but who introduce modern practices and ideas quite casually in the course of living.

"Now that [our helper] Dodo is here, I'm relieved of the drudgery of washing 150 milk bottles every afternoon. The milk cooperative is succeeding in respect of enough customers and in the handling of the milk. We have taken the bold step of forming a legal cooperative, with some falling off of milk-bringers, who look at the twenty-one lei monthly dues they must pay, rather than their 800 to 1,000 lei monthly profit! We've also raised the price of our milk from seven to eight lei, with consequent loss of customers, but a necessary step, as it brings us 400 a month more to cover all our labor and expense. So far we've born the brunt of the whole thing—initial investments of over 8,000 lei, broken bottles, the early days when a whole shipment turned sour."

Jancsi knew the customers' doors by memory and stopped at each of his own accord. However, Mihai, the driver, was not only pocketing part of the profits, but using the wagon to joyride his girlfriend. One day he brought a load of glass bottles to a tragic end in a ditch. Because we were teaching and demonstrating the cooperative, we took the losses upon ourselves.

Added to our losses was the fact that the rocky Meszko pastureland was dry that summer. "Our milk supply has dropped alarmingly," I wrote home. "We found that, over and above the cost of oats for the horse and Rozsie and Mihai's labor, we were earning just three or four dollars a month for living expenses! And yet if we are to have this cooperative at all we couldn't ask the peasants to bear their share of expense in the beginning. They are so conservative, cautious, and suspicious.

"Then we found that Mihai, the Romanian boy, had put over 2,000 lei into his own pocket. Even harder on us is the fact that he is the laziest thing alive, and our garden and fields have suffered. We fired him, whereupon he softened our foolish hearts with a day of alternately violent weeping and singing. His second trial is over, though, for yesterday evening he sauntered cheerfully into the house with the scythe and large reports of all the grass he'd cut, but when Feri slyly suggested that they go together with the wagon to collect the grass, he had to confess he'd spent the afternoon with his sweetheart. It's hard to find anyone to take his place, and we're not sure what to do."

At a critical moment in the life of the milk cooperative, Terus came to Meszko. A tall, strapping Jewish woman, her beauty was well set off by a heavily embroidered Romanian dress. Terus had grown up in a Saxon town in a Romanian mountain district. I had met her by chance at Cook's Travel Bureau in Vienna. English-speaking people were rare in Transylvania, and Terus told me in English that she had just spent three years in England getting a doctorate in agriculture.

"Oh, you're just the person to help us!" I exclaimed. Terus spent many evenings doing cooperative planning with Feri and many days tramping from village to village, giving expert advice, watching the details that make the difference between success and failure. As manager, she moved the milk cooperative to another village that had first-rate pastures in the middle of the valley.

At first the villagers laughed at the milk cooperative, which meant such work and a loss for us. They thought we were fools. But out of all these efforts eventually grew a highly successful cheese and butter cooperative. Other villages followed suit and by 1934, a streamlined cooperative store for valley produce had been established centrally in Torda. At that time the cooperative had a regular market of ninety members and 400 quarts of milk daily. As for us, the store eventually returned our losses and labor in the form of all the butter and cheese we could consume.

To cut the Hungarian wheat in the flatland, the Mokanys, an ethnic group of Romanians, traditionally came down from their mountains and worked in exchange for bread. The men wielded long-handled scythes, the women hand sickles. Like everyone else, I sent great baskets of smoked bacon, bread, and wine to the fields.

There were a few private threshing machines in Transylvania, but they were not always accessible. We believed that harvesting grain could be better accomplished by a cooperative threshing machine. When Feri discussed the idea with his newly formed Agricultural Society, they were receptive. Both Hungarians and Romanians to whom we talked individually were ready to join the project. "It is difficult to know whether to organize it so as to admit Romanians at this early stage, or not," I wrote to friends in America. "Eventually these two peoples must come together, but at present there are individuals among the Romanians who are ready for opportunities to oppress the Hungarians. They are hardly to be blamed, for the Hungarians did the same to them when the Romanians were the underdogs."

At the last minute, the local Romanian priest told his people, "Don't have anything to do with a Hungarian machine." The Hungarians went ahead, with hopes of state aid. Not to be outdone, the Romanians came together for the first time and bought a bigger and better threshing machine. Five Romanians pledged themselves as guarantors for their machine. They were counting on state aid, which was always denied to any minority undertaking. Thus our village, which could have been ably served by one threshing machine, resounded with the racket of two. The smaller Hungarian machine had the advantage of being able to scuttle over and around alabaster outcroppings where the heavier Romanian thresher got stuck. Hungarians would chuckle softly when they heard the Romanians straining and cursing to free their machine.

The Romanians came out on top, however, as officialdom was on their side. Cooperative equipment was supposedly free of taxation for three years and then taxed only lightly. When Feri went to register our machine, the official held out for a huge bribe, almost as big as the tax on a private machine. Because Feri refused to pay it, he was sent on bureaucractic wild-goose chases. There were also internal troubles with our cooperative machine. All went well during the first year when Feri was in charge of purchasing and bookkeeping. Then he turned the job over to the villagers. Their elected manager bought bad oil and twice as much gasoline as necessary, gave short measure, and replaced good wheat with poor. Only Feri's intervention prevented the villagers from sending him to prison.

Then the state seized our machine for taxes. Twelve villagers loaned 5,500 lei to get it back, plus 2,000 to pay as "commission" to the state agent. The twelve then turned upon the village and demanded the entire profits for the year as interest on their loan. To check their greed, Feri put up the money himself, with the understanding that it would be repaid from the year's profits, but also that the machine would recoup its loss by working for neighboring villages. At harvest time, however, an outside machine came and undermined the loyalty of some of the villagers by charging one percent less than our machine. Funds were insufficient to repay Feri as well as the newly accumulated tax.

Once more Feri went to the state agent, who asked for another bribe. To complicate the picture, some Romanians had reported the 2,000 lei "commission" as the bribe that it truly was. In response, the Romanian gendarmes descended upon the givers of the bribe, instead of the taker!

Weary of all the trouble, half the village said, "Let the threshing machine go." The other half had become attached to it, however. "No! Our little machine has become used to this hilly village!" The debate went on and on. Several Romanian villages, however, eventually followed the example of Meszko and became cooperating owners of threshing machines. We felt that our small beginnings in cooperative undertakings had been successful, at least in pointing the way.

When I lay in the hospital reflecting on the loss of my baby, it seemed to me that if the immediate cause was influenza, the deeper cause was the physical and economic insecurity of life in the village. We had just learned that the state payment to the Unitarian Church had been reduced by one half. By our first Christmas in Meszko, Feri was doing four times as much work as one man should. Although tired, he was considering a lecture tour to pay our debt for the *Britannica*. I was worried needlessly, it turned out, as he didn't have time to go lecturing after all.

I felt strongly that I did not want to bring a child into the world in light of our economic conditions. I wanted to see our $750 debt paid off, so that all of Feri's monthly salary could be ours. The debt wasn't overwhelming, but paying it off gradually from our income would take several years. I didn't want to wait three or even two years for another child. By early 1931, I was seriously considering a return to America to find work and pay off our debt. I was also deeply lonely. I thought the best thing would be to return that spring and try to find a teaching position with a progressive school (a move Feri opposed). On the other hand, living expenses might eat up a considerable part of my salary.

I thrashed it out with Aunt Isabel and Uncle Mellen. "My interest just now is not really so much in schoolteaching as in broader social and religious questions. If there was any hesitation about my decision to marry, it was the desire to go deeper into the study I began with Dr. Sharman. I have far to go before I am satisfied with my understanding of the New Testament. If I were 'on my own,' I think I should prepare to teach in this field. . . .

"We have made small beginnings—almost nothing in face of the need here—yet significant as beginnings. To meet the immediate financial side of our problem, Feri and I could make a series of photograph lantern-slides, enabling me to tell American Unitarians about the life of Unitarians in Transylvania. I could earn part of my expenses by selling some lovely peasant jackets.

"Naturally, Feri hates to see me leave him, and uses many arguments against it. He thinks I'm unduly concerned about money, and that we'll 'get along somehow.' Being a man, he does not feel the loss of the baby as keenly as I. Nor does he know much of the difficulties of housekeeping and cooking under primitive conditions and economic limitations. The time is soon coming when I will need more clothes. Later, I can spin and weave lovely woolen material for dresses, suits, and coats for both of us, but it takes money to invest in a few sheep and a loom!

"All too ready to forget about our limited funds when it comes to the village, Feri comes home without the woolen gloves he MUST have for winter, because they cost $2! While in many ways our life thus far has been idyllic and thrilling, it's too close a nip-and-tuck for my peace of mind. . . .

"You say that we have 'borrowed too much.' You may say that I should not have gone to China because it eventuated in borrowing from Dr. Sharman. It was a glorious chapter in my life and I came out the richer for study with him, wherever it may lead. As for Feri's borrowing from the church, what else could he do? Ill, no money of his own, having been put into that high school for something like $3 a month salary? The thing that proved foolish was the purchase of the *Britannica*. If we had been able to use it for the purpose for which it was bought, it would have paid for itself. . . .

"I understand why missionaries are usually sent out for periods not less than three years. It takes at least a year or more to 'break through the ice' of a foreign country and begin to enter into the language and minds of the people. Shall I then remain here for another year or two, until I have mastered the language and entered more deeply into the life here, or should I come sooner?

"I have a feeling that many little difficulties, such as the outdoor toilet in mid-winter, are in a gradual way undermining my health. . . . I'm not risking any more baths in this drafty house until my cold is all gone. . . . I don't go to church anymore, either, because there is no stove. . . .

"On the other hand, perhaps my worst troubles are over. We have persuaded the village to restore this ancient church in its historic beauty and simplicity rather than build an imitation of a modern, citified type. This may leave about $600 in the treasury. The village is so taken with our idea of a Community House that they may, if enough money is left over from the church, build us a new house next fall and turn the old house into a Community House."

If I stayed, I knew I'd want to have a child in about a year. I was desperately lonely, without people of like interests to talk with. Although I had many friends in the village, I had no real friend. Even though I walked, read, and tried systematically to study alone, it wasn't enough. Feri and I were one another's company too much. Partly because Feri also had no adequate friend in the village, we shared more with one another than most married people. Yet two people cannot eat, sleep, and live in one room way off in a tiny village without needing new and fresh currents.

I wanted a child, but not in our present house. Even in a new house there still would be conditions in the village unfavorable to a baby's health—open toilets, manure piles, and flies! Yet *if* we could afford a screen porch and took the most scrupulous care? Feri was not as optimistic as I about educating the village on open toilets and manure piles.

My inner practical Dane counseled me to settle down for the long haul with patience, and to stop being torn over the inadequacies staring me in the face, especially those which could not be remedied. I couldn't help feeling frustrated and angry. I kept thinking of what we might do in Meszko if we only had the means. The things we were trying to do were the things any young American "missionary" to a foreign land got paid at least $75 a month to do. If only there were some group to back us with even $25 a month for village education!

"Would it be premature for me to come to America next year, to speak to Unitarian and perhaps Quaker churches?" I continued in my letter home. "Feri thinks I'd be better justified in doing this four years from now, when we've achieved something substantial. I maintain that our achievements will be more substantial if we have a minimum of security for our own life. Besides, four years from now I want to be embarked on raising my family. Also, I think we *have* already achieved something here!"

"I don't think I'd be happy leaving Feri unless absolutely forced to, so now we'll try to weather it for another year, and see how it goes," I wrote to my cousin Catherine. "As for my health, I can't say yet with much certainty how I am. I haven't great faith in doctors here. I didn't want to come home because I was ill, but I knew that if I continued in the conditions that then existed, I might undermine our whole future here. Sometimes flight—if temporary—is wiser than fight. At present I am anemic, rather easily fatigued by physical labor, but able to do a moderate day's work with an hour's rest in the middle.

"As for the sort of spirits I'm in, I find it a great relief to have come to a decision, and am throwing myself into gardening for all I'm worth. My greatest difficulty is loneliness. I'm like a tree who has lost some of its good roots in the transplanting. I hope I may be sufficiently tree-like not to mourn lost roots, but to sprout new and equally strong ones as soon as possible."

Within a few weeks my mood improved, despite the dull grayness of the winter. Hardly any snow fell that year, and there was mud a foot deep in the village roads. (*Sar van!*) I could feel spring coming.

That spring of 1931, something else lifted my spirits—the Bagge family in Torda. Mr. Bagge was the director of a large cement factory and also the Danish consul. Although big, bluff, and kindhearted, Mr. Bagge was a capitalist type, skeptical of the educability of peasants. He visited me when I was in the hospital with the miscarriage, bringing chocolate, books, and bananas as rare and expensive as roses in December. Mrs. Bagge was cordial and lovely, with frank blue eyes, an intelligent and gracious person. They both spoke English. Mrs. Bagge had studied in America and visited Berkeley. We discovered that Mrs. Bagge's cousin had been Feri's cabinmate on his voyage across the Pacific and his traveling companion in Japan.

Like many Danish houses, the Bagge home was beautifully crowded with fine rugs, books, pottery, etchings, and paintings. It even displayed a row of blue Copenhagenware plates of the same pattern we had at home. It gave me such a happy yet homesick feeling when I saw those plates on the wall.

With its blessed uplift, spring finally came. To whet our appetite, my father and stepmother Olga sent new agricultural bulletins. Two came in the nick of time for pruning fruit trees and growing gooseberries and currants. The trees and bushes on our place had been neglected for years. I found pruning exciting, especially on young trees whose form and strength I could determine. I enjoyed the idea of "going forth" to our own fields. Although in many ways I was a mere play-peasant, our close connection with the soil was in dead earnest.

"If I could plan an ideal life for myself," I wrote my father, "it would combine teaching and studying at a university, raising a family, and living in a country-like place where one could garden, keep animals and bees, and carry on some sort of handwork for avocation, such as weaving and pottery. To have them all at once would be Utopian; but one must rather make the most of whichever aspects can be present at one time. Right now for me, it's garden, animals, and handwork."

In addition to its usual bounty, the summer brought news of a forthcoming visit from my old friends and benefactors, Antioch College president Arthur Morgan and his wife Lucy, for me, two of the most intelligent and delightful people on earth. Once when I was ill at Antioch, Mrs. Morgan took me into their home. Whenever I didn't know what else to do, I used to go to her. Since some of my letters from Transylvania had fallen into her hands, the Morgans had become very interested in our efforts.

Protagonists of "the small community," Mr. Morgan was a Unitarian and Mrs. Morgan an active Quaker. He had become impressed with Feri's social imagination, and she with the fact that for the past two years I had bought only two pairs of stockings and a flannel nightgown.

The Morgans' visit couldn't have come at a better time. "Days pass now like the flowing of a stream, busy and without great event," I wrote Aunt Isabel in midsummer. "Now and then I inquire what the day of the month is, but with only one interest, the approaching visit of the Morgans. . . .

"We are in for several days of downpour, and welcome it is, after the long dry period. The ground has been hard as rock, with such deep cracks, we could neither weed nor hoe in the garden. Today I hoed the strawberry patch and put all the new runners in order. We didn't get a berry. The chickens ate them all because we couldn't afford a fence to keep the wretched creatures out!

"Feri has gone away for an all-day assembly of district ministers and school teachers. He wanted me to come too, but, to the privacy of your ear I must confess I'm bored to death by the ministers and schoolteachers I've seen, the so-called, self-called 'intelligentsia.' Dull. No spirit. Maundering through a traditional 'job'. . . . So I stayed home and planted lettuce.

"It saddens me very much, the narrow fixity of desire and interest here. I wish Feri were not connected with a church. I wish he were free of those ancient formulae. He's full of ideas and purposes, wears the harness lightly and is pulling his own way, but if he should ever settle down in the traces! He has to do and say things because people expect it. Although he is never insincere, he is not himself. If he were, he wouldn't be bothering with much that is required of him now.

"I guess I am less tolerant than he. He is absorbed and happy, but I cannot help wishing that he were working with a group of intellectual and spiritual equals or superiors. I want him to develop personally as well as to help others develop. He needs the criticism and stimulus of such association. So do I, more than anything else.

"I feel that my life has come to a standstill. I'm physically active all day, yet inwardly chafing. I'm like one of the bean vines in my garden that's waving round and round at the top of its pole, or perhaps has lost the pole part way up.

"A person must relate truly to the life that is in him before he can relate truly to the life around him. Now that I am almost out of 'civilization,' now that I have been living in a community which lives in its present and acts on its impulses, I'm developing a passionate interest in culture. . . . I've learned to fear raw human nature here. I've seen village boys drunk and quick to pull out their knives, and villagers shouting at the top of their lungs in a public meeting, abusing each other over petty differences of opinion or personal grudges. I have to learn to not turn away depressed, but to see evil as just a negative thing, in light of man's positive potential.

"To top things off, I tripped in my own kitchen and broke a preserve jar! A spear of glass was driven an inch deep into the sole of my foot. I pulled it out, pressed the wound firmly, washed and put iodine on it, and when Feri came home, went to Dr. Kovacs. It is healed now, but if I'm on my feet for long it aches.

"Feri is thinner than I like to see him, and recently had a week of inexplicably high temperature. We haven't the strength to be farmers nor the money to pay others to do the heavy work."

When it seemed I had reached bottom, help came providentially. I received a job offer. Through my cousin Gonna Bredsdorff, a liberal Protestant minister in Denmark named Torkild Skat Rordam asked me to come to Ryslinge at his expense and help translate his lengthy life work—a "scientific" critique of New Testament sources. I would live with his family and be paid $18 per month plus $85 at the end of the two or three months of work. Gonna had suggested me because of my study with Dr. Sharman in China. Utterly delighted, I accepted Pastor Rordam's offer. I began studying Danish by myself, with occasional help from the Bagges.

"It's just the kind of rest and change I need," I wrote Aunt Isabel. "Besides earning money to pay off our debts, I can get better acquainted with my relatives, including sweet old Uncle Otto, as well as visiting the college, folk high schools, and cooperatives.

"Oh, I'm hungry for the amenities of civilization, and will enjoy them to the full. Food, bathtubs, and people with whom one can talk! It seems providential, coming so unexpectedly just at this time. Rozsie and Dodo will housekeep in my absence.

They know how we like things, and there will be over 200 jars of preserves to feed Feri. Feri wishes that he might come to Denmark too, but not with debts on our hands!"

The other big event of my summer that year was the Morgans' long-awaited visit. One evening their American car came bumping over our alabaster rocks. "Those long-horned oxen—I was afraid they'd puncture my tires!" said Mr. Morgan as they pulled into our courtyard. Mrs. Morgan began to unload their car, packed full of all the things she'd imagined we might need. "*Istenem*! (My God!)" said the villagers, "we didn't know anyone had so many clothes!"

After making an inventory of my meager kitchen equipment, Mrs. Morgan took me on a shopping trip to Kolosvár. There she had her first experience of eastern European shops, swarming with hand-kissing clerks who had but few of the things she asked for. After a night between hemp sheets, Mrs. Morgan insisted on leaving her supply of cotton ones. "Just in case of guests," she said, when I tried to refuse them. Unobtrusively, Mr. Morgan slipped something into my hand. "Give it to Feri after I'm gone," he said, "I notice he doesn't have one." It was his watch, "a spare," he insisted. Another of their gifts was a big copper kettle, an absolute necessity. After they left, we preserved kettles full of tomatoes and delicious plum jam. Even with no sugar, the jam kept all winter.

Two little neighbors, Rozsika and Lena, spent most of their waking hours as helpers at my house.

Because Mr. Morgan was a professional engineer, it didn't take him long to discover that Meszko was gradually falling into the river. Why we were so cold in winter and why our tile stove smoked so badly were apparent. Our kitchen had parted company from the living room to the extent of a three-inch crack in the floor of the doorway. The trunk of a giant oak farther up the hillside was slowly being torn in two. Jula Neni's porch actually stood a yard away from her house. Fed by each spring's melting of snow in the mountains, the Aranyos River had been eating into the hillside, gradually cutting away ground from the nearest gardens and houses. There was a year-round downward dislocation of the hill.

When the roar of the swollen river could be heard all over the village we had some exciting spring nights. Sleep was interrupted by tolling bells. Lanterns bobbed along the paths, converging at the scene of danger. Men tore down tiles and hacked away window and door frames from willow and clay walls in an attempt to save part of a house before it collapsed into the flood.

Crude efforts had been made to protect the hillside. Loads of rock were placed at the base of the hill and bound by woven willow fencing and newly planted trees. The state had been prevailed upon to give money to build a concrete retaining wall, but the sum had disappeared somewhere between Bucharest and Meszko. With his experience in flood prevention, Mr. Morgan proposed doing away with the most devastating curve of the river by cutting a new channel. Feri put it up to the village council: If the people of Meszko would give a little spare time, the work could be accomplished. However, since it was chiefly the Hungarian half of the village that was in trouble, no move was made. Mr. Morgan also suggested increasing the parish income by irrigating the Kopta. His engineering office in America even prepared blueprints. Again, only a hope and a paper plan.

The Morgans tried to find an American market for Hungarian peasant pottery. This project was difficult because of the extreme irregularities of hand production, official red tape, and export taxes. A few thousand lei was gained, however, from exporting alabaster vases made by Meszko craftsmen on their footwheels and decorated with designs I adapted from ancient Greek illustrations in our *Britannica*. Mrs. Morgan took some embroidered children's dresses, leatherwork, and samples of pottery to show at the Unitarian headquarters in Boston.

With a little smile, Mr. Morgan paid off our remaining debt on the *Britannica*. As a young man, he had also bought a set before he was affluent enough to afford it. The Morgans even loaned money to the Meszko church to build us an adequate house. Mrs. Morgan commiserated with me regarding Feri's urge to throw all our resources into social objectives, risking health and family life. Listening sympathetically to Feri's complaints about my yen to return to America on a money-raising expedition, Mr. Morgan told us about the depression's effects on charitable giving. They offered to help us get more support from America by writing about our work in *The Christian Register.* If their efforts succeeded, it might be our economic salvation. Even more than the Morgans' aid was the sheer joy of talking with supportive friends from home.

When they returned to America, Arthur Morgan reported to the American Unitarian Association: "There is a small group of young ministers in Transylvania who, I think, are undertaking a rather remarkable piece of work. These young men have studied in America and combine a modern critical attitude with an intense religious interest, a combination not too common at any time or place.

"The leading spirit among them is Balázs Ferenc. In India, he found young men talking volubly about saving their country, but using most of their energies in theorizing. In China, he found a group of young Chinese, each of whom had picked out a small village in which to work. Here they were teaching the people to read and write, to practice better methods of agriculture and in general to achieve a new cultural level. Balázs felt his sympathy to be with the latter. He has come to the conclusion that regardless of the country Transylvania belongs to, the same work needs to be done.

"These young men . . . are in a position to bring their communities almost at one step from a medieval to a modern life, without intervention of generations of past prejudices and superstition. . . . It would be of great promise to eastern Europe if there were a center of high moral quality and intelligence from which leadership could spring. This region is one of the critical points of Europe. Peace in the Balkans and in Europe will not come by formula or panacea but only by the development of intelligence and character."

Mr. Morgan discouraged the thought of my coming to work in America for a year. He said it would be like a "little divorce" and that I'd probably come back to Feri's funeral. I felt intuitively that the Morgans' visit and my forthcoming journey to Denmark marked a new epoch in our lives. In keeping with that, it seemed appropriate that we move into a new room, the one which the Morgans had occupied. It was lighter than the others, with two windows to the north and one to the east. We wondered if it would be warm enough for Feri that winter, with three outside walls. However, it was smaller and easier to heat.

I wanted to leave for Denmark shortly after October 25, the day our renovated church was to be dedicated. However, I could not leave until I got a Romanian passport from Bucharest. My American passport and citizenship were set to expire in April 1932. I wrote to Aunt Isabel, "I feel most gloomy at losing my citizenship. It's because of the American law that a woman married to a foreigner must revisit America every two years, which is only possible for the rich."

Meszko was near enough to Torda so that town standards visibly affected folk traditions in the village. It was seen in the most obvious externals, such as clothes and glass jewelry sold in the street fairs. The dream of every village girl was to have a pair of artificial silk stockings to go with her one dress of printed cotton of town style, even if her father had to sell the pig to buy them. On weekdays, this girl was a barefoot lass in full homespun skirt and kerchief. On Sunday, she enjoyed the luxury of shoes and a handkerchief.

Her elders were not very different. Churches hundreds of years old, with beautiful wooden balconied towers, hand-hewn beams, carved pillars, and ceilings charmingly painted in colored folk designs were being torn down and replaced by modern atrocities created by small-town builders, using sheet iron, ornate gin-

The old tower for the Unitarian templom came down during renovations.

gerbread, jigsaw carving, and gilt paint. Such was to have been the fate of our templom. Although quaint and lovely, it was sinking dangerously to one side. The villagers had been saving money to rebuild it. We considered inappropriate their plan for a modernistic addition. With much tact, patience, and persuasion, Feri gradually brought the villagers to see the historical value and architectural beauty of the church, a pure Magyar style perfected over many centuries. At first we were told that the church was between 150 and 200 years old. However, from some ancient, worm-eaten records we discovered that it dated to the end of the thirteenth century.

The men of the congregation worked hard on the restoration, hauling gravel with ox carts and reinforcing the brick, stone, and mortar sanctuary wall as well as replacing the old tower. Debreceni Laszlo, a young architect whose mission was to travel about Transylvania preserving and restoring ancient bells, towers, and walls, spent many days with us making the plans for the renovation. Feri spent almost all his waking hours for about three months directing the project and doing much of the labor. It gave me shivers to see Feri painting the many-colored designs on the ceiling, with only a narrow, shaking plank between himself and destruction.

The renovated church was beautiful, its painted ceiling a chant of joyous color, and the pulpit, pews, organ, and columns of the galleries all with little carved, colored designs. The galleries were painted in Magyar designs similar to the ceiling. The woodwork of the pulpit was especially impressive, with its parts cut and locked together.

On October 25, 1931, we dedicated the *Meszko Templom es Orgona Avatas*. When automobiles full of guests from Torda and Kolosvár rolled in, the pride of the villagers was complete. A history of the restoration had been prepared. A high point of the ceremonies was placing the record in a hollow metal ball, which was crowned with a wreath and carried by one of the young men of the village to the top of the tower and set in place. More than two hundred people came to the dedication, including the bishop, an Englishman named Mr. Drummond, several professors, and the best historian and archaeologist of Transylvania. Everyone thought it the most beautiful village church in the country.

Respite in Denmark

Not long after the church dedication, I left Meszko. "I shall stop off . . . in Budapest with Feri's sister," I wrote Aunt Isabel, "then Vienna, to meet the Quakers to whom Mrs. Morgan spoke about our work and needs; Prague, to see good friends; Berlin, where a friend from Dr. Sharman's group is doing graduate study; then Copenhagen, to spend a night with dear old Uncle Otto; and then to the Rordams in Ryslinge, on the island of Fyen."

I spent a week with my uncle. Though blind and seventy-six years old, Uncle Otto had good health and a wide-awake mind. His son lived within walking distance, and several friends read to him every week. While I was there my elderly aunt Maggie Frederiksen came to meet me. She was much interested in my tales about Romania. I also spent a couple of days at the International College, which I had visited two summers before.

After the seventeen-day journey, I was ready to settle down in the Rordams' charming thatch-roofed parsonage. I enjoyed the food immensely and loved exploring the gently rolling countryside every afternoon in the company of Stryck, the Rordams' dog. The solid comfort of the fat, orderly farmhouse and barns prompted poignant comparisons with the poverty I had left in Meszko.

Although I had left Feri behind, he was always with me. He wrote, "I feel as if I were . . . just about to be flooded with happiness, when everything vanished. I lie on the ground with the staggering knowledge: She is gone . . . aching all over, restless all the time for want of you, shivering outside the closed door, unable to regain poise." In spite of such letters, at that moment, Denmark—far from Meszko and Feri's pain—was for me a brighter and safer world.

Pastor Rordam was modern and well read, with a ready sense of humor. A large man, he would have looked well in the priestly frock of the middle ages. In Mrs. Rordam I found keen intelligence and charm. To my father and stepmother I wrote, "Pastor Rordam utilizes all my waking hours, with the exception of a short walk in the afternoon, to expound his theories and plug along with me through the technical Danish of his book. 'Skat' is a delightful man, about fifty-four years old, but with the habit, all too common among ministers, of delivering long discourses without giving his hearer a chance to get a word in edgewise and assuming that one does not understand when one merely disagrees. His father had been bishop in Copenhagen and was held in high regard by Uncle Otto.

"The book we are working on promises to be interesting. Rordam believes it to be radical and revolutionary. He says that if my English is precise enough for eventual publication he will give me twenty percent of the proceeds! But whew! It is an undertaking. I've got to steep myself in the English and Danish vocabulary. We get along well together. He seems satisfied with my readiness at interpretation and my ability to type."

Skat and I worked for about seven hours each day together. Often I continued typing into the night. At first, we held long theological discussions but finally agreed to limit them, since time passed and we accomplished nothing. My conceited little hope about my own possibilities as a synoptic scholar shrank to almost nothing, yet the fascination did not leave me, nor did discrepancies between Dr. Sharman's and Skat's work and views.

Despite Feri's anguish in my absence, providential was the way I felt about Denmark. This word also described a heretofore hidden reality, one that promised great joy. Soon after arriving in Denmark, I discovered I was pregnant.

"Dare I tell you?" I shared with Aunt Isabel in February of 1932. "It's most thrilling and exciting, and though you may think I have not business to be, I'm thoroughly delighted. . . . According to all the little books on the subject, the critical time is past. My wee babe is now almost four and one-half months old, and all the attachments are firm and secure. Last night I felt what I'm sure must have been some little kicks. It was the sweetest feeling, coming so unexpectedly from the middle of me, evidence that the tiny one is really there, lively and energetic.

"I sleep twelve hours out of twenty-four, go on walks, drink plenty of nice fresh buttermilk, and feel and look very well. I visit a good Danish doctor in the neighboring town. . . . The babe arrives the last of June, and the charges of birth, doctor, two weeks of hospital, and all, will not be more than $40 if all goes normally, as I have every assurance now that it will."

Feri at first insisted that I return to Meszko to have our child, or at least soon thereafter. "Seven months will quite do to live apart, and *I want to be no stranger to my babe!*" he wrote me. "If I had to be deprived, for the sake of a safe delivery, of the most lovely and precious time . . . when you have the babe within you, I will not be deprived of a month of its growing life."

He finally promised to come in time for the birth. He had been busy writing a village diary, which *Helicon*, a prestigious literary and publishing society in Transylvania, wanted to publish in book form, paying about $60. He hoped to use the money for the trip. I thought a visit to Denmark would also be useful for Feri, that he could benefit from a summer's study of Danish cooperatives, and make connections with the People's College. Peter Manniche, married to my cousin Emmy Louisa, had heard good reports of Feri's work in Transylvania and offered Feri a lectureship for the coming year. To my disappointment, Feri responded that he could not leave the village for a year, because he didn't want to lose ground.

"What I shall do next year is still uncertain," I confided to Aunt Isabel. "I cannot risk taking the precious baby back to that cold, old house and inadequate income. The state has made still further reductions in our monthly salary, so instead of $9 a month, it is $5! There is some hope that money may come from America for a new house, but there is not time next summer to build it.

"I keep thinking that I should be doing something next year which would either let me earn a little money or give me definite training for life in the village when I go back. If I can only have the means to make a good home, a good school, and the desperately needed baby clinic and day nursery, then I'll be busy and useful. Eventually, we'll get the necessary support from America."

In light of approaching motherhood, I felt that my satisfaction in life would come from more practical work. To be happy, I needed to feel that I was really accomplishing something. It was depressing to live in the midst of desperate need and not be doing all that I might to help. I thought of getting some training in Denmark to help mothers in Meszko learn how to take better care of their babies. The doctors in the district were doing nothing then in the way of such education. I wanted to visit the seven villages in our valley and hold baby clinics, sending cases that required medical training to the doctor. Since it was difficult to persuade the people to go to a doctor, I would need to be able to treat the commoner illnesses. As I thought about it, next year seemed to be a good time for such training, which would be one of the greatest contributions I could make in Transylvania. Yet I realized Feri was feeling increasingly lonely and jealous of Skat.

"Dear Kriszi," he wrote. "I consider your idea of getting all sorts of training a kind of rationalization, how you explain to your conscience your reluctance to come back. Think me selfish—but then, think it out plainly—what are you? . . . You have to see that it is not training, equipment, success, that will make you happy, but some *genuine change* in your mental outlook.

"Kriszi, you have to understand that it will not do to prolong your stay in Denmark beyond September this year [1932]. . . . If the baby arrives on or about June 20, you can expect to be strong by the middle or end of July. We would have about six weeks or two months, if I decide to be home by about the middle of September. Why, in two months we could visit all your relatives and learn all that may be necessary or possible by way of housekeeping or day nurseries.

"I tell you, it's no romance to live without you for such a long time. And *you* can bear it all right? My cold fish! Oh, Kriszi . . . I am not mad, only lonely and melancholy. If the economic factor is so important, perhaps I should not go to Denmark at all—who knows whether I shall earn anything by articles?—but rather, pay the book debt and the church. . . . Sweet Kriszi, lovely Kriszi, do you really love me one-tenth as much as in America?"

Feri seemed incapable of understanding why I couldn't bring a baby back to the conditions in Transylvania under which we lived, where we had no dependable and decent income. I had lost our first child under those conditions.

Feri wrote, "So far we have not spent anything on clothes, etc., but for the village. . . . You say we were in utter poverty. Well, that's a bit too much, when there are millions in the world unemployed, who have not even a sure place they can live. It is rather hard to believe, being the kind of person that I am, that your happiness depends on *material things*. As long as we were above the poverty line, and we were, I thought you were the kind of person that lived on one's own spirituality. Believe me, if you could not be happy with me, the village, and Transylvania, you will not be happy even if we would have a huge income. *Money does not bring happiness.*"

I shared my exasperation with Aunt Isabel, begged her to intervene. "In a cold and conventional world one *has* to make allowance for a certain minimum of clothes and mundane necessities. And if housekeeping is to be more than the most depressing drudgery that will make me an old woman before my time . . . I must have a certain minimum of equipment. I'm not going to be embarrassed by borrowing certain simple household articles, or delaying payment on things like eggs from my neighbors any longer.

"Please make him realize the utmost importance of a certain minimum of economic security, from the point of view of health, strain on nerves, and bringing up a family. . . . He is indignant that I am 'setting conditions,' and that I want some assurance of definite income. I am just as ready as he to live like a 'lily of the field,' up to a point; but lilies cast forth their offspring without responsibility in a fashion impossible for humans. And he can't count on your $10 a month as a cornerstone for our life! If he feels he must stay on in the village for the sake of his work, well and good. I'll do all I can to help him, but then he's got to let me go for a year, without protest.

"He writes such nonsense about 'money not bringing happiness.' Heavens! As though I ever thought it did, in itself, and ever wanted much of it. . . . Feri is busy writing, lecturing, organizing—the work he loves and is fitted for. He has no conception of the drudgery, fatigue, and privation involved in trying to keep house under primitive conditions. . . . Feri has not yet tried to see things from my point of view. He's one of the finest persons I know, but blind, utterly oblivious to certain things."

At that time, I missed my mother terribly. I continued, "I suppose it's natural when someone marries and goes away from home and has many new fundamental experiences, to reflect and wonder if her mother or her aunt ever encountered such problems and what they thought and did, and what sort of a 'philosophy of life' they've arrived at! One can't write about it—it would make a book—while in talking, one talks volumes without knowing it."

I felt that I would bear a girl, and the prospect gave me comfort. If Little Boo was born in Denmark, although she would still be a Romanian citizen, a girl would be automatically exempt from the Romanian draft.

After hearing that Feri's meager salary had been effectively reduced to $2.60 each month, I put out several lines for employment in America for the coming year. Emma Cadbury of the Friends International Center was going to visit Feri in April, and I hoped that the Quakers could offer us some help or advice. Then the Morgans sent disappointing news about Boston Unitarians' supporting young Transylvanian ministers. Any such relationship had to be between the official church headquarters of America and Transylvania, not with individuals. There was little chance for improving our situation, in light of the narrowly dogmatic and ecclesiastical character of the Transylvanian church. Despite all this, I was feeling physically very well, and cheered that snowdrops were out. Every day Stryk and I walked in the beech and pine forest on Fyen.

When she got the news of my pregnancy, Aunt Isabel wrote quickly, suggesting that I come back to America for a while. I replied, "I don't feel alone in the world any more! To think of seeing you again! . . . And I feel such a sense of comfort and satisfaction that you know about this baby, and take a share in advising me. Because you *are* my family, and one only has to be away from one's relatives for a while to learn how precious they are!"

Of course Feri adamantly opposed the idea of my going to America for any reason or length of time. "I have given up having plans in connection with you. . . . Suppose I become obstinate, you would either come back in a state of mind that is not fit for anything, least of all for a happy life. . . . I make arrangements for a 'bachelor's life.' I will take no steps to build the new parsonage. Personally, I can get along very well in this room, and see little reason to make an effort."

On March 2, 1932, he wrote, "Your letter . . . just came. It's a lovely letter, perhaps the loveliest of all. My letter, written perhaps at the same time, is perhaps the nastiest of all. Yet I am not sure which of the two has the right thing to say. You settled down to a life sweetened by the thought of a baby and its father (funny to be called so!) and feel very complacent and benevolent about it. I begin to believe it means the end of a lean attempt to get rooted in Transylvania. You really are so happy now that you think you'll be just as happy after coming back, especially as the date is put in such a far away distance that it does not really trouble you yet. It is not real. You protest against my idea that you'll want to go to your other life every year or so. Yet you seem to be happy only if and when you are away . . . the longer you stay in the western world, the more impossible it will be for you to be satisfied with Transylvania. If you think you can just pass a year or two (Denmark, England, America) without me, quite easily, it should be easy for you to do without my visit this summer. . . . You remember the idea was that I go out to see you and come home together with you. I promised no visit otherwise."

I had not thought of being separated from Feri for a lengthy time, not for more than a year. Aunt Isabel's mention of coming home for several years filled me with a sort of panic. I finally agreed with Feri that living apart was "no marriage."

"But it is also 'no marriage,'" I wrote Aunt Isabel, "to be struggling along in Meszko on next to nothing. . . . If one is reduced to peasant conditions oneself, one is worse off than a peasant, because they are used to it. There's a Danish proverb, 'When there's nothing in the manger, the horses begin to bite each other.' For the ultimate good of our marriage itself, we ought not to subject it to a strain which might reach the breaking point. Better to separate and join each other again when it can be happiness to do so. The greatest difficulty is that Feri is satisfied to go on with things as they are. . . . I suppose he thinks that if there have been babies who have survived being born in a manger, his will be one of them!"

I couldn't decide if Feri was a saint or a fairy or a little boy. "Whatever he is, he needs somebody to take care of him, because he's too busy taking care of Transylvania to even buy himself a new toothbrush or shoes and stockings. . . . He's a sweet, adorable person, and not a dreamer. Far from it, when it comes to the work he is doing there. The great thing I fear is that he'll sacrifice himself prematurely. Self-sacrifice in the long haul is all right, because then there is a long span of accomplishment to justify it. . . . Feri sees human need so acutely, it is his own undoing. That's the worst thing about my going to America. If I go, how can I be sure that Feri will be taken care of? . . .

"Feri assumes that whatever he can stand, I can. He identifies me with himself. However, I am first of all, me; secondly, a woman; and thirdly, an American. . . . No, first of all, I am a fellow human being, and therefore have great interest and sympathy for everything that concerns him and Transylvania, but the other factors have to be reckoned with."

My relatives must have thought I was a bit mad, having a baby in the face of such personal difficulties as well as a world economic crisis. Our struggle was taking place in a world moving closer and closer to major conflict. "I can't escape an awareness that the present state of affairs is most threatening," I told my father after hearing more about Adolf Hitler's rise to power in Germany. "The narrowing of vast economic control in the hands of a few, the large-scale, impersonal manipulation of funds without concern for the individuals affected, the ancient tendency to exploit other humans for material advantage, plus the terrific power of modern chemical and mechanical techniques of war.

"There's Romania, a country of poverty-stricken peasants . . . squeezing the people to the utmost . . . all for military purposes. I get letters now with a new postage stamp of a huge battleship with menacing cannon. The Copenhagen paper came out with the theory yesterday that if Russia sides with China, Poland and Romania will leap into the fray on the side of Japan."

By staying in Denmark, I thought I could make the most of this chance to bear a child in a civilized country, under good living conditions and with freedom from physical strain. My salary was not enormous, about $8.50 a month, but I was hoarding it for the birth of my child. Where I would go from there was an open question. Mrs. Morgan had written that "the American Unitarian headquarters have rather completely let us down." Miss Emma Cadbury, head of the Friend's International Center in Vienna, said that the Quakers were feeling the strain of the times and couldn't offer much help. The American Friends Service Committee had its hands full and couldn't help us.

Despite the economic difficulties, I wanted this baby very much. I thought how terrible it was to have to choose between one's husband and one's baby. Yet I knew I had to take care of myself for the sake of the baby. So there really wasn't much choice, short range. Feri had his village—his greatest absorption and joy—and I had my baby. For the immediate future I decided to put the baby first, since the first year was the most important one for establishing its health. I was willing to return to Meszko the following summer in 1933 only if we could build a good house and have enough income for physical necessities. Under those conditions, and with knowledge and vigilance, I believed I could take care of the child, offsetting the disadvantages of the environment.

My decision to return to the village was partly based on a perceived change within Feri. At least, I thought I saw some small beginnings of a new understanding and I had not lost faith in his continuing development. "Maybe if I love him enough he'll grow to be less oblivious," I hoped. The sojourn in Denmark had given me a perspective beyond the extraordinarily difficult circumstances of the past two years, which were enough to wreck many marriages. Our relationship still seemed sound and worth trying to build on. If only we could get more help with the threatening elements of our life.

I was encouraged and impressed by Feri's prolific work in my absence. Increasingly he seemed to be winning interest and respect, not only in Romania but in Hungary as well. Feri was on a committee that drafted a petition to the Romanian parliament to get the cultural autonomy for Transylvanians accorded by the League of Nations. He had been invited to go to Budapest to give radio lectures on Gandhi and Tagore. *Helicon* magazine had published some of his articles. Of all the samples submitted by Unitarian ministers for a new book for religious education in the Unitarian schools, Feri's was chosen. He had also written a small book on his philosophy of religion. Some of his poems and articles about our folk school for village youth appeared in Budapest newspapers.

Feri had succeeded in getting the people in the villages of our valley to cooperate in supporting an agricultural adviser—a real accomplishment. Next was to attract a doctor and public health educator for the valley. His accomplishments hadn't yet brought much income, since pay for writing was low. But they were full of promise.

I wrote to my father, "Many of Mother's, Isabel's, and your prophecies have come true with regard to Romania, but that must be offset by the thing I saw and held to from the very beginning: that I married an uncommonly fine person who bequeathed, I hope, something of his intelligence, character, and creativeness to his child. If he doesn't work too hard and undermine his health, and if the Romanians don't sit on him (which we hope to avoid by keeping out of politics and trying to help Romanians as well as Hungarians), he is going to be an influence in the whole of Transylvania. So don't be gloomy on my account, Father, because whatever life may be, it's frightfully interesting."

During the final days of my pregnancy, I was working on Skat's manuscript, playing croquet, going for walks among beautifully ordered gardens and small parks with lilacs, hawthorne, and pink water glories, and just sitting by the sea. I moved to my Uncle Otto's for the final wait. We were sitting on a log in Charlottelund when I began to feel rhythmical pains in my back. It was 5 P.M., and the baby was on her way! By 8 P.M., when water came suddenly, I made tracks for the Rigs Hospital in Copenhagen.

I was examined by the *Ovedr-Jordmor* ("Head earth mother"—in olden times, the one who lifted the baby up from the earth for the inspection of the father, who determined whether it was worth keeping). By 9 P.M., the pains were coming every five minutes, so to make them come faster I walked for an hour. At 2 A.M., they were every three minutes, but not quite hard enough, so I walked more until they were so strong they doubled me up. Suddenly I was in the grip of a whirlwind or an avalanche, doubled up like a hinge. The pains came fast. I pushed like a demon. Boo was born at 7:30 A.M., June 11, 1932.

When a Jordmor said, "I see hair!" it was like "Land, ahoy!" A multitude had assembled and was scurrying in all directions. Up to this time I had been the object of their attention, but now it was all directed to the little one. I felt suddenly *de trop*. You might as well chloroform me, I thought, and they did.

A faraway voice was saying, "It's a girl."

I heard my own faraway voice as though it didn't belong to me, "Is she all right? Is she healthy?"

"Yes, she's fine!"

Turning my head, I saw a little crimson creature, flinging her arms and legs in all directions, protesting against the first contact with soap and water. That first glimpse of dark hair and forehead was of Feri's child, beyond a doubt. Presently I was put on a stretcher and a little bundle was laid in the crook of my arm. I was so relieved and happy to think she was here, healthy and normal. I had seen poor tiny babies in Romania die soon after they were born, but I could see that mine wasn't of the dying kind. She weighed six-and-a-half pounds.

To name the baby, Feri proposed Enikö, an ancient Szekler name, pronounced "Onikeu," the last syllable like the sound in the French *boeuf*. I later called her Enika. Feri's objections notwithstanding, after recovering from childbirth I interned for a month at a small maternity hospital in Copenhagen, learning medical procedures so that in emergencies I could do similar work in Romania. One day I was fitted with a pessary, a birth-control device.

From Feri came disturbing news. "I absolutely refuse the thought of your lingering and staying away any longer than necessary, now that you've finally decided to come home. This is on health grounds just as much as on mental grounds. I've written to you several times about my hardships in caring for too many things. I was facing nervous breakdown at one time. This small temperature may not be the result of mere physical strain, but also of the impossibility of handling kitchen, garden, fields, new maid, and books all alone. . . . It is just stupid to stretch this visit beyond nine months. We may mean to live together, but all the time we seem to be separated. Ours is a letter marriage."

Still I procrastinated. "Dearest Bogy," I wrote home, "I am back in Ryslinge, but not living with the Rordams. . . . Feri is getting desperate in his longing. He is alternately begging and commanding me to return in September, but I don't see how I can until the work is finished. He wrote an adamant letter to Pastor Rordam, who sent a nice reply explaining how the work stands. . . .

"I'm afraid to leave Feri alone in Meszko much longer. He is just so lonely, it has affected him nervously and he feels he can't stand it any longer. Mr. Bagge wrote to his wife that he thought I should come back to Feri as soon as possible. So, I guess I must return to Romania this winter. Same old story with Feri, undernour-

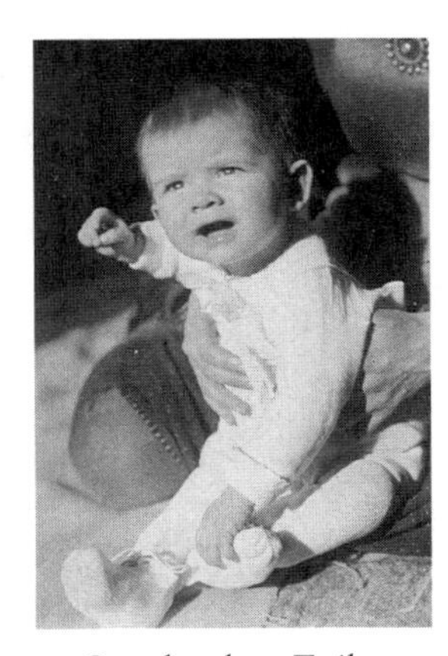
Our daughter Enika.

ishment and overactivity. He is very weak, feels it is a crisis in his health, and asks me to come. There is no new tuberculosis for him.

"I'll try it for another year. Then if conditions are no better and help doesn't come, I'll strike out elsewhere and take Feri with me! The New York church which sent the marvelous box of baby clothes asked if they could help, and I've just written them a long letter. If we can live decently and I can have the means to make a really good school for those village children, I can be happy, provided I can escape out into the world now and then!"

I reflected on the future of my child. If she should show any talent for music, I wanted her to have the best teaching Romania afforded. I had my eye on a fine creative school in Budapest. And the three of us, if Feri's lungs could stand the jolting, would ride horses for days at a time, so that she would know the country thoroughly. I was still worried that Feri seemed bent on staying for years, trying to improve the village. Yet his longing and his health could not bear having me on some other part of the earth. As I planned my return to Meszko I still had many questions, including: How compatible are freedom and marriage? On December 10, I left Denmark for Romania.

Despite my misgivings, I was glad to be with Feri again. I found things somewhat better in Meszko . . . a promise of a raise in our salary and our house showed improvement. Having rugs on the floor and decent wood to burn made a great difference in keeping warm. We established the small but brightest room for the baby and me and a larger one for living, dining, and Feri's study. The kitchen, the biggest room, still contained in usual peasant fashion the loom and the maid's bed—a custom I didn't like, but there was no other place.

Our fourth room was given over for community purposes. There the village women met to spin and read, and folk high school classes twice a week, and children on Sunday afternoons for games. All those things Feri took on himself. We were able to serve tea at some of our community gatherings, after finding that we could manage our food for three adults and the baby on $10 a month.

I found the misery in the village more appalling than ever. Shortly after returning, I went to the home of a Gypsy family to take some milk for their baby. I found a house of one room, broken windows stuffed with newspaper, a pathetic little stove, dirt floor, two beds with loose straw and a few rags, and a chest of drawers. Five barelegged children huddled close to each other for warmth on the beds. The sack of old children's clothes I brought with me from Denmark helped so little! Most villagers considered Gypsies worthless. However, I could not sit by and see human beings living worse than animals. The Gypsy children were bright. I was convinced that if only some teaching could be given them, they could live differently from their parents.

Hungarian peasants had so little with which to help others, as their own children wore everything to rags. Many peasant families were undernourished and underclad, such as Albertine, a mother of ten who less than a week after her last baby was born was up and struggling with housework. When I visited, she had just crept into bed with her boots on under one thin old blanket. The house was so cold, the tiny stove couldn't keep it warm.

Returning as a new mother and reentering the life of the village, I found much to do and less freedom to write long letters to family and friends. Taking care of the house and baby took most of my time.

On February 11, 1933, I wrote to Aunt Isabel, "What shall I tell you about my baby, in whom I live, move, and have my being? That she is sweet beyond anything I ever knew? Feri remarked that she 'is the last word in loveliness'. . . . Sometimes she might be called beautiful and sometimes homely. She is gaining in weight again, and with the coming of spring weather, will make up for the period of whooping cough.

"Feri is now in the last lap of the influenza, which has hit Transylvania with the same vengeance it is showing in England and elsewhere.

"Your description of the depression in America fills me with a certain irony. When there are so many undernourished children in this village, it is curious to hear of American youngsters who give Depression Dances and deliberately cut up cloth to make patches for a dance costume! Most of the children here need those patches in dead earnest to keep the wind and snow out of the rents in their one or two ragged garments. I'm in favor of some form of government which will allow everyone the bare necessities.

"We shall have a little boy, Rudi, living with us for the next three months, in order that he may go to school. He is a miserably undernourished waif—spindle legs and pot belly—half-starved by an incompetent, drunken grandfather who has kept him alive by begging. But he is a sweet, bright youngster with sensitive features, blue eyes, and freckles. We found him in a deserted house, unable to go out for lack of clothes and shoes, and alive thanks to occasional hunks of *polizska* from Romanian neighbors. We cannot do otherwise than take him in, as we have enough food in our cellar and barn."

After Rudi came to live with us, it took him time to believe that three meals could be relied on. He hid leftovers under leaves in the garden, all but burying them like a little dog. Nails and other small articles disappeared, to be found later hidden in the barn. "He's a thief!" scolded Agnes.

We commissioned Agnes's tailor-brother to make Rudi a suit out of an old one of Feri's. To get rid of the lice, we shaved his head and stood him in a wooden tub with water as hot as he could bear, scouring every inch of him. In a week, however, we were at it again, using kerosene on his head and baking his new suit in the outdoor oven. After going through the performance several more times, Agnes exclaimed in disgust, "It's no use. He was born with them!" Rudi believed her until finally we got rid of the lice and he was able to go to school.

"Now I am going to be a little gentleman!" he cried blissfully. Agnes was quick to disillusion him of such presumption.

For three weeks in the fall of 1933, Aunt Isabel and Uncle Mellon shared our little one-room thatched house in the hilltop orchard. They found it as charming as I had hoped. Their visit filled me with emotion. Once when we were alone, Isabel implied that I was complaining too much. Her words hurt and made me realize how nonsensical is mentioning one's private anguish to anyone else; although to speak of it may prove a help and relief.

Aunt Isabel also criticized me leaving Enika alone for an entire morning to read. I thought it a misunderstanding and later wrote to her, "I was entirely at fault for having left her, I know. I did not realize that she was ill. And it was not for the 'reading,' it was for the wonder and marvel of you and Uncle Mellen being there. Two of my own people, of my own country, who stand for things. . . . It was you, your voices, every least thing you did and said I was alive to in a way you can never, never realize, you who have not cut yourself off from them for life in another country. . . .

"I often wonder whether I should not have kept to myself the hard things about this life here. I remember your saying on one occasion that I shall never be happy again! That of course is not and must not be true, any more than my exclamation, 'I cannot stand it!' Of course I can stand it; one simply does, and without much effort, when it seems to be the ultimately right course.

"I can only be happy with such a treasure of a baby as Enika. As far as the difficulties . . . I can only do the present job as well as I can. As you said, one never knows what the future may bring, and one must keep mentally and spiritually alive so as to be ready for whatever may open. If there are losses, there are gains. The longer I stay here and my real understanding of people grows, the more I admire the Hungarians and feel myself with them. There's bound to be an overwhelming sense of loss at times, but it should eventually be compensated by an equal sense of gain in the insight into another people and another tradition, and in the effort to unite the best of one's own and theirs. I am not unhappy, and you must not be for me."

Just when we thought our house building would have to come to a halt for lack of funds, a letter came from Mrs. Morgan with a hundred dollars enclosed. She wrote that they knew from experience that a house always surprises one at the last by needing more money than one could reckon for.

During the winter following Aunt Isabel and Uncle Mellen's visit, our little house at Meszko became a discussion center for students. They would ski across the hills from Kolozsvár, to delve honestly and deeply into their attitudes and traditions. At those gatherings we encouraged Agnes to participate, and she could carry her share in conversations as easily as she could carry a basket home from the fields. Another of the few women who participated was Erzsebet. A keen and vivacious student, she was a new experience for the Tanito, who always joined us. Erzsebet argued up and down with Kovacs, who loved it.

Around this time, the *durva* or harsh side of Agnes, which Feri had noted from the start, was coming more and more to the fore. I thought it was because of her father, and she encouraged me in this belief. Her intolerance of Rudi increased, while she became intensely devoted to Enika, too much so, I sometimes felt.

"She's the only person in the world that I love," Agnes would cry, as she snatched the baby from the crib, kissing her toes. She would sing her classics of Hungarian babyhood.

Where were you, little lamb?
Where were you, little lamb?
In the forest, my lady.
Who beat you, little lamb?
Who beat you, little lamb?
The bad shepherd, my lady.

Agnes thought I spoiled Rudi by climbing up to the hayloft each night to see him safely under his horse blanket and say goodnight. The focus of Rudi's love was likewise the baby. His face would light up as he sang:

> We must go to Debrecen,
> We must buy a turkey cock,
> Look out, the wagon is rickety
> and full of holes,
> The turkey cock will fall out!

Rudi possessed an extraordinarily beautiful singing voice. He had a wide-ranging repertoire from singing at fairs, from angelic songs about the Christ child to lyrics such as "Come on in, radio repairman, I'm all alone in the house." As Agnes's harshness to Rudi increased, I found him passing on his resentment to Donkee, twisting the poor beast's ears and poking his private parts with a stick. Donkee retaliated by more frequently running away with the water cans.

One day, Feri brought a piece of news that made Rudi's blue eyes shine. "The minister of the next village plays the violin. He had to sell his, but says he'll teach Rudi if we'll buy him one."

"I've heard a violin can cost as much as a cow," warned Agnes. Rudi shrank deeper into his corner, hugging his knees fearfully.

"We have no money right now, Rudi," I said, "but Agnes is going to sell our potatoes in Kolozsvár, and then the Tiszteletes Asszony will see if she can find a second-hand violin."

Agnes and I drove our wagonload of potatoes over the long, bumpy road to Koloszvár and slept all night on her place in the market square. She was a hard bargainer, but potatoes were everywhere. She was only able to sell the wagonload for 500 lei. While she was at the market, I shopped around for a violin, finding that one would cost 8,900 lei! Since I had to stay over in town for a few days, I commissioned Agnes to tell Rudi how the situation stood, with the promise that he should have his violin in a few weeks.

"Where's Rudi?" was my first question to Agnes upon my return to Meszko.

"Disappeared, Tiszteletes Asszony. I told you he'd be ungrateful."

Rudi had vanished. His grandfather had been seen talking with him on the outskirts of the village. Two days later, without a word to Feri or Agnes, he had gathered his few belongings, including the toothbrush he said was his "best Christmas present" and which he used proudly every night. I suspect the grandfather wanted Rudi to try to earn money for him by singing. My feelings about Rudi's leaving were mixed. The grandfather was a drunken crook, and I was afraid Rudi would become like him. On the other hand, it was a relief not to have to combat the perpetually reappearing lice. Rudi cost us more than we could afford.

Some weeks later an old man told me, "I heard the child yelling, and looked in the barn and there was Agnes, beating him and pulling his hair."

"Have mercy!" I cried.

"Mercy nothing. He thinks he's going to get a violin, but the Tiszteletes Asszony is never going to get him one," the old fellow responded.

As long as I remained in Transylvania, when I visited market places or fairs, I hoped to see Rudi again and make good to him on my promise of a violin, but I never found him.

Climbing a Mountain

Common among the villagers, especially if it was a question of cooperative undertaking, was the comment, "*De rosszek az emberek!* (The people are bad!)" It always seemed to be "the people" as separate from the speaker, with the implication being, "It's no use considering whether this is a good idea, since my neighbors are too untrustworthy." The belief also covered an inordinate fear of gossip. Whom to talk to and how much to say were real questions. However, conversation was the main outlet for curiosity, emotions, and power. No wonder the villagers pried, dramatized, exaggerated, and embroidered.

Fatalism was another prevailing attitude, both in a religious and common sense. Flowery sermons on immortality left the people skeptical. "Where shall I go when I die? In the ground." On the dearth of the grape harvest one fall, a Romanian peasant shook his head sadly. "It's the penalty we have to pay because the ministers mix in politics."

One of my first lessons in the Hungarian mindset was the statement, "*Nekem bolham van* (To me there is my flea)." "To me there is" suggests an unalterable fate. Likewise, the common phrase, "*Ugy van* (so it is)," was indispensable to a philosophy of endurance. To the Transylvanian Magyars, there had been too many fleas and heavy burdens. "Life is hard" at least meant the struggle with scarcity, exacerbated first by Turkish depredation and later by Romanian encroachment.

On a national scale, this attitude was expressed in song and conversation about the "*Szegeny Magyarak*," the "poor Hungarians" of tragic destiny. Their unreasoning, fiery patriotism seemed to have come down from the warriors whose portraits still hung in places of honor, or from fifth-century Hun ancestors who ravaged and pillaged Eastern and Central Europe until they finally decided on settled life. Historically, there had been little regard by nobles for peasants or by Hungarians for neighboring ethnic groups. "*A Toth nem ember!* (The Slovak is not a man!)" was commonly heard.

My first experience of Hungarian-Romanian hostility had been on the day of Feri's inauguration to the Meszko parish. As part of the ceremonies, he passed under a festive arch of pine boughs, with red paper flowers tucked among the greenery. Next day, the young men responsible for decorating the arch were hauled before the gendarmes, threatened with prison, then let off with a fine. I couldn't understand the offense until I admired a woman's new house of whitewashed walls, red tiled roof, and green window frames. "Magyar colors!" she whispered, gratified that I noticed.

In some districts the gendarmes were more vigilant than in others. A friend wanted to give me her Hungarian costume, beautifully embroidered in many colors.

"But I can't take this," I protested. "You have put days of work into it; it's your holiday dress."

"I don't dare wear it anymore," she said sadly. "It has too much red and green."

Personal relations with our Romanian neighbors were always friendly, however. We went regularly to pay our respects to the Greek Catholic priest, a tall old patriarch with shrewd blue eyes and a white beard. He regaled us with his cherries and asked many questions about America. He told us proudly about his son studying geology in England, and showed us his collection of stones, fossils, and broken pottery from Roman times.

The priest's daughter, a faded wisp of a woman, was alight with kindly interest, and begged us to come more often. I admired her weaving and embroideries with their exquisite and sophisticated use of geometric forms. She always served us the customary tiny portion of sweet jam, to be eaten with a spoon. However, her husband and his companion, a dark and brooding character named Juge, were unapproachable, beyond the most superficial politeness. Feri regarded Juge as "the evil spirit of Meszko." The two men kept the policy of "Romania for the Romanians" alive in the village.

The attitude of Kovacs, our Hungarian schoolteacher, toward his Romanian counterpart was propitiatory. Although they made formal calls and drank together, Kovacs figured the Romanian aim was to create one state school. Hungarians were required to refrain from working, not only on national, but on state church festival days as well. Thus, even after droughts and much-needed rain, sometimes the farmers could not take advantage of ideal conditions for weeding, cultivating, and harvesting, but often were forced to fret at home. Gendarmes patrolled the fields. Many a day I had counted on help, only to be met with flat refusals from Agnes or Jula Neni. "We don't dare. They fined Daco Sandor 300 lei, and Rozsa Neni got five blows on her bottom!"

Once when a group of Hungarian youths were planning to put on an evening play, that afternoon Romanian gendarmes, without explanation, gathered about forty Hungarian men, the play's hero included, and marched them to a city five hours away. Just as we were wondering if the play could go on, our hero appeared. He had managed to get an auto and tear back in the nick of time.

In larger villages, each house had to display the Romanian flag and burn candles in the front windows. Often on holiday nights, groups of Romanians milled about the streets, shouting threats to Hungarians. When one group armed with clubs and stones menaced a special candlelight service in our church, Feri urged the congregation to keep cool, thus averting a battle. We did not go unscathed personally, however. A rock thrown through the window of our house made a gash in the opposite wall. After that, I kept the baby's crib out of range.

During several evenings of hostilities, Feri again acted as peacemaker, this time in a fight between drunken Hungarians and Romanians. I wrote to Aunt Isabel, "A small band of Romanians were waiting in the dark street with knives. One with a revolver under his coat commanded Feri to see that certain Hungarian young people were sent home from their dance. There might have been bloodshed, but Feri managed to bring a peaceful outcome. Afterwards, he had a week of fever."

At that time, Benito Mussolini had been on the radio advocating the revision of the Treaty of Trianon. He issued free railroad tickets to Hungarians and invited them to immigrate to Yugoslavia. Strong feelings against Hungarians flared up among Romanians all over the country and mass meetings were held. On one such occasion, Romanians were called out of the mountains for a day of stirring speeches in Torda. On the way back that evening, their train suddenly stopped at Sinfalva, the village across the river from Meszko. A load of drunken peasants led by the Greek Orthodox priest's son-in-law surged through the streets. "Here and here," he said, pointing the mob to attack Hungarian houses. Our friend Arkosi, the Unitarian minister of Sinfalva, fled with his wife to the church tower.

A few hours later Feri and I saw the wreckage—men in bed with broken bones and bloody heads, animals beaten and turned loose. Mrs. Arkosi was in tears; her house was a shambles. Everything portable had been carried away. The valley was in an uproar. It was rumored that the whole Romanian district was inflamed and would descend on the rest of the Magyar villages. There were gruesome recollections of 1848, when Romanians had been incited by Austrians against these same villages, when babies, it was said, had been tossed onto bayonets. Worried Meszko women set about burying their valuables in their orchards.

Mr. Bagge sent his carriage from Torda to bring us to safety behind the walls of the large cement factory he managed, but Feri insisted on staying in Meszko. That Sunday he gathered his Hungarian football team together and for the first time challenged the Romanians to a game. Intrigued by the novel opportunity, they played together, and nothing further happened.

As time went on, treatment of minorities became increasingly oppressive. There were frequent petty retaliations on the part of the Hungarians. Once the Romanian mayor of a nearby village was driving in his sleigh, his Christmas tree tied to the rear. When he reached home he discovered that the top half of the tree had been cut off. Another official had taunted some Hungarian youths, "You needn't sing like that. You haven't got a country to sing about!" Angered, the young men struck him, killing him by mistake, they said. I visited the boys in prison after they had been beaten and drenched with buckets of ice water by the gendarmes.

A Hungarian lawyer from Torda told us how his profession was forced to allow a few Romanians to dominate the Transylvanian central legal committee that admitted new members to the bar, thus excluding many Hungarian candidates. He and other Transylvanians were kept out of a lawyers' conference in Bucharest by the Iron Guard, a Romanian vigilante group. Eventually the few Hungarian students in the universities who had hurdled the deliberately tricky examinations were terrorized. The Iron Guard even cut off the ears of a minority professor.

Mr. Bagge was in despair about developments. In his dual public roles, he had taken a personal stand against bribery, an institution on which most business in the country depended. "But he could not hold to it," Mrs. Bagge told me sadly. Years of compromise had left him embittered.

An additional Romanian move was to place in every industry a government official with the power to hire and fire. A rule that seventy-five percent of the workers in each industry must be Romanian resulted in the importation of inexperienced

Romanians into purely Hungarian districts, thus depriving many communities of their livelihood. Hungarian peasants mining their fields in Meszko were forced to employ their Romanian neighbors. There was little to show for the excessive taxation of Transylvanians. When the Romanian monarch, King Carol II, came to visit Meszko for a few days, a huge sum was spent to construct a racetrack for his amusement while roads remained unspeakable.

I never became accustomed to the gendarmes coming to our home to try to discover the real reason for my being in the country. Once in the middle of the night, I dreamed that I was talking to some men, only to awake and find myself sitting up in bed, actually answering the interrogations of three gendarmes. I shared these disturbing developments and other observations with my family and friends in America. Lucy Morgan was on the point of sending some of my letters to *The Atlantic Monthly* for possible publication when she was warned against printing anything detrimental to the Romanians, since it might make matters worse in Transylvania or endanger our position in Meszko.

Just after we came to Meszko, Feri wrote this poem, a promise, a love song to the village, a declaration of faith and intention. With his abilities, he might easily have gone elsewhere, taught at the seminary in Kolosvár. But he chose a village where he could demonstrate his beliefs and try out what he had learned about community, cooperation, and improvement.

> I stop here. Here I shall remain.
> I shall put down my roots here
> and not depart till my ideas have come
> to blossom and the bearing of fruit;
> the winged seed may indeed fly further.
> Or, if my effort should fail, should decompose
> and remain sterile, without life,
> then over me shall pass history's plough,
> turning up and later revealing
> what is required.

In his effort to fulfill his promise, Feri encountered hurdles of poverty, ignorance, superstition, and the state repression. He had to deal with the resistance, conservative tradition, and bureaucracy within the Unitarian church. Feri and I were becoming thorns in the flesh of the church hierarchy in Transylvania. Most of the problem was Feri's social theology. He was frequently pestered by the central church headquarters with one false accusation after another—especially of communism and humanism—apparently to find some excuse to remove him. The only valid claim they could make against him was that he was honest, independent, and straight-spoken.

Aniko Szantho Harrington, another Transylvanian Unitarian minister who later became my close friend, described Feri's theology in her essay, "Under the Clod—The Life and Work of Francis Balázs."

> When Francis arrived in Meszko, he found [that] people . . . believed in a God . . . who rewarded good and punished evil. Yet they saw also that very often the evil seemed to reap the rewards, while the good were punished. This they wished to change by prayer to God. When this did not work they often became unbelievers.
>
> Francis saw God as the natural, unifying process of all life, including men. He believed that man's role was to create community. The goal of life, and therefore of religion, was to continually increase the sense of community within each individual's consciousness, and in bringing all of the individual consciousness together to bring into being a "beloved community" based on love.
>
> Religion, as he saw it, was not separate from life. . . . Religion is not just knowing that God exists, religion is doing something about it. Religion is seeing the whole Universal Process and incorporating [one's] whole life into its service.
>
> God, he said simply, "is the soul of the universe." The universe is alive. Its soul is what makes it what it is, and has made and guides every creature, from the smallest to the greatest. We cannot know this God fully, for it is mysterious and beyond our knowledge. Yet we can see its marks and evidences all around us, on every hand.

Many of Feri's beliefs and actions distressed the Unitarian church conservatives, notably the Reverend Boros Gyorgy, Bishop of Kolosvár. When Feri published an article in support of humanism in his magazine *Keve Kotes*, it was the final straw for the bishop. Soon afterwards, on January 6, 1934, he wrote a letter to the dean of the Unitarian District of Torda:

> We have found ourselves in considerable trouble lately with these conceited young ministers like Balázs Ferenc and one or two others. Balázs has proved many times that he is not for the ministry but is rather a humanist educator of the people.
>
> He profanes the Unitarian pulpit by wanting to live and pray without God. However much I respect his goodwill and although I give him credit for having made better and more beautiful, first his church and then his parsonage, I realize from his article published in the *Keve Kotes* that spiritually he is [more] equipped for American license. . . . The foundation of our [church] constitution is belief in God, and its consequence is divine worship on the basis of the Gospel of Jesus.
>
> Whoever sees that "for a large part of humanity, the existence and idea of God is without significance" and wants to help the situation by wanting to make man a Humanist is no longer a Unitarian minister and is not worthy of this title.
>
> To build a life of faith in our Transylvanian situation surpasses Balázs Ferenc's spiritual equipment. . . . He is more radical than the English Unitarians. At best, he could have discovered proper ground in America. . . .
>
> I call upon the leaders of the Aranyos Torda district to call Balázs Ferenc to account for his beliefs . . . to make clear whether he can and wants to be a Unitarian minister on credal ground. . . . Let the Dean and the Lay Curators of the district examine whether Balázs Ferenc does not do more harm than good, and, under the cover of the Unitarian ministerial gown, which gives him great authority, is he worthy to continue his mystifying and without doubt, destructive work.
>
> If the result of the first questioning should lead to that to which Balázs Ferenc has referred: his readiness to stand before church court trial, the leaders of the district shall do as they think best, and report the result.

Feri stood trial before the church elders in Torda in the summer of 1934. Earlier he had met with the bishop and the Presidential Council. According to Bishop

Boros, "We called him to task . . . and enlightened him as to the fact that he walks in mistaken ways." Feri answered their questions, albeit not as they would have wished.

"The Unitarian authorities are . . . making themselves ridiculous, in fact, trying to put Feri out of the church," I wrote home. "They summoned him to a most medieval inquisition, bishops and all. The rest of them perched on their throne-like chairs, but Feri, as an American Unitarian visitor put it, 'was too smart for them.'"

At the time of the trial, Feri was sick. We had spaded and raked a big piece of garden, Feri shoveling manure, which overtired him and resulted in a severe attack of bronchitis. He was in bed for two weeks. Even with a fever, he got out of bed and faced the church fathers. Postponement of the trial would have prevented his getting a passport in time to attend the upcoming World Congress of Liberal Religions in Copenhagen, where he had been invited to give a lecture.

Feri had to go to Bucharest to apply for the passport. He spent two months trying to get it, making about twenty journeys to Torda and Kolozsvár, buying countless stamps and collecting numerous documents. At last, expecting the passport to come at any moment, he packed for the congress. Then word came that yet another document—our marriage certificate—was needed by the passport authorities. He had to take it to Bucharest, with all the influence he had plus that of a Romanian fellow in the PEN Club, an international writers' organization.

In addition to his lecture, Feri took part in an international symposium at the congress, speaking briefly about Transylvanian Unitarianism. His old mentor and president of the California Unitarian College in Berkeley, Dr. Earl Wilbur, was also on the symposium, which was broadcast over Europe. The already strained relations between Feri and the church hierarchy were made worse by his participation. It was a blow to Bishop Boros that Feri had been invited (all expenses paid) and was asked to give the presentation on Transylvania. The bishop had written to the chair of the congress that he wanted to give the symposium talk himself, but was refused. (I'm afraid I had a small part in it by writing some frank letters to people in Holland and America.) When Bishop Boros threatened not to perform the ceremony of final ordination for Feri, Dr. Wilbur said, "Well, if they don't, we will!"

Despite the furor at home, Feri's talks were well received. Dr. Charles Joy, vice president of an American Unitarian organization, asked for a copy of his lecture for *The Christian Register*. Later I learned that Dr. Wilbur had told Bishop Boros that it was impractical for his seminary to accept students from Transylvania unless they would have adequate positions upon their return home. Dr. Wilbur wrote, "My urgent advice is to keep on taking students from Transylvania, because the villagers need help of a range and content, and vitality which the official church . . . is incapable of giving."

Following the trial and the congress, the church fathers continued their surveillance. In November, leaders of the Aranyos district sent Feri this questionnaire and directive:

> Is your soul satisfied with the God-conception of the Unitarian Church of today so much so that you dare to take upon yourself the task of proclaiming this sincerely and with conviction? Are you willing to break with those ideas of yours which, according to us, are mistaken, dangerous for our church, and are imported from abroad?
>
> How did you dare to criticize so rudely, almost nullifyingly, the Lord's Prayer . . . declaring that "It is probably a lie on the lips of most Unitarian ministers" and "Most intelligent men either do not use it at all, or if they do, symbolically."
>
> Make a sincere and unevasive confession of your religious belief, and declare . . . without rascally sophistication, whether you wish or are able to be a Unitarian minister on *creedal* grounds.

Feri's quotations were taken out of context in such a way as to falsify their meaning. His thinking was that certain words in the Lord's Prayer have to be taken symbolically rather than literally.

In addition to being old and of a narrow bent, the elders were probably worried by anything that might ruffle the feathers of the state, which contributed to the Unitarian and other denominations. As Bishop Boros wrote to the district dean, "The present time is not appropriate to discussion of matters of dogma. Still less is it fitting that our ministers should publicly publish . . . thoughts which give opportunity to those who are old hands at it, to doubt that Unitarians are Christians."

There were two sure ways for a minister to win popularity in Transylvania. He could play oratorically upon personal grief until the women of the congregation wept audibly. Or, more effective with the men, he could play upon national hopes and hatreds, with frequent allusion to the "poor Hungarians." Feri felt that this unrealistic faith in political or military miracles weakened people's grasp of the present and discouraged the development of their own resources.

In her essay, Aniko Szantho Harrington best describes the fine line Feri walked in his Meszko ministry.

> Francis moved through his village and the people were touched and changed. Not that this was easy, for they had deep-set, traditional ways of doing things. But he was himself the first to step forward in doing things differently. You can't leave everything to God, he said. God needs helpers in this village. Who will help me build God's kingdom in Meszko?
>
> The village people wished him to care for each family and each person individually. Rather, he tried to bring them together in groups to tackle their various problems. But the people often resisted.
>
> From time immemorial the village pastor had cared first for the well-to-do, the rich landowners who had the biggest houses. Francis spent most of his time with the poor peasants, the small landholders and the landless ones who often had the largest families, the least education, and the lowest income. This did not sit well with the rich and powerful, some of whom withdrew their support.
>
> Opposition developed with the church. Once forty men refused to come to the church and to take communion. Then [Feri's] voice faltered. He reexamined himself and his goals, asking, "Who am I, and what am I trying to do here?"
>
> His answer . . . was that, as a clergyman, he was fulfilling the cultic needs of the people, but also and even more important was his prophetic role. It was his task to speak the truth to his people even if it was sometimes unpleasant, and challenge them to live more justly and generously with each other. He felt he must be the village's living conscience, who would show what was good and unsparingly condemn what was bad. He had to be the leaven, the fermenting agent, to help bring the Kingdom of God to Meszko.

> My destiny is this:
> to be understood by a few.
> In the lives of some
> to be a leaven.

For many others
to be a goad.
I carry, however,
the seed of the future,
not the present's broken
and bloody body.
—Francis Balázs

Feri urged his congregation to cooperate with Romanians as individuals and neighbors, though not necessarily with Romanian policy. He risked his popularity within the parish by pointing out Hungarian weaknesses, such as extravagance of emotion and lack of practical initiative and social concern. Feri paid a steep price for speaking out. He even became unwelcome in his sister's home in Budapest because he had voiced the heresy that there were good Romanians.

My departure from village ways proved costly, too. "I've been hearing a lot of things people say about me lately," I wrote Aunt Isabel, "such petty things, mostly trivia and nonsense; not things you or I might consider my *real* shortcomings. My democratic attitude, efforts at friendliness, and my work and play with the children have lowered me in their eyes because I have not maintained the 'kiss my hand' aloofness of the conventional minister's wife. Terus [manager of the milk cooperative] says I'm too nice to them and give them too much leeway. It's very difficult."

I had to admit that at least one of the charges the church elders lodged against Feri was true: He was indeed eccentric. That trait, when combined with his stubborn refusal to see other points of view, weighed heavily on me. One time I especially experienced his stubbornness during the winter of 1933 to 1934.

"Isabel, . . . We are moved into the new house against my will. The front hall, through which we must continually pass from kitchen to living room has no secure ceiling or floor, only a few loose boards thrown across. The toilet is not made and the front hall has no door or windows put in. Feri just would not wait, and I was in bed with a cold and slight temperature, too. Terus was furious. I said I would consider moving in when the front hall was fixed. Feri starts some men 'fixing' it with those loose boards, believing that it will be ready by night, and while I'm sleeping, moved all the kitchen furniture in.

"Mrs. Bagge was here the day before, and begged him not to think of moving in this winter. She felt the kitchen was damp, as well as the difficulty of an unprotected front hall through which we must continually pass. But Feri took both her remarks and Terus's as interference, and was obdurate.

"He simply rides over anything I say. Terus says he is difficult to work with. He expects too much of people, is a 'dictator' and wears people out with sheer argument so that they finally yield from weariness. I agree with her. We tried to tell Feri these things but he won't listen, gets angry, thinks us unjust. Terus was so indignant about the whole thing that she sat out on the kitchen table last night and sobbed. I had my weep yesterday morning and Agnes, hers this morning!

"It is a puzzle, this hard will in Feri, because he is otherwise a splendid and gifted person. He just grants me no quarter. There is something merciless in him, something rigid and unrealizing. His attitude about this whole thing is that Terus and I are the stupid, unyielding ones, that I do not have consideration for him. It was the same during that whole year of argument by letter from Denmark. He did not budge an inch from his position that I was unreasonable in 'setting conditions,' wanting to be sure of an income and proper housing for the baby.

With Feri and Enika in front of the Meszko church.

"He disregards things that I ask him to do about Enika. He takes her into the kitchen of the teacher's house, where the teacher's old mother continually coughs. I ask him please not to give her grapes, because she is still too young to manage the skins and seeds, and he goes right ahead, and the only way I can check him is to become very angry. Yet he adores Enika, and she loves him. It is a puzzle!"

"*De rosszek az emberek!* (The people are bad!)" Agnes declared emphatically. She had cut our field of hemp with a hand sickle, hauled it to a swampy lake, and sunk it deep in the mud. Now, weeks later, it was "retted," soaked to separate the fibers. She waded in up to her chest and dug the filthy bundles out of the black muck. After whipping them repeatedly in the river, she spread the stinking mass against our fence to dry.

"The people are bad like this hemp smells," Agnes elaborated. "Gossip, gossip. You never know who you can talk to, or how much. Curious like magpies. Nothing in their lives to talk about, so they must make talk."

A few days later, the hemp's smell had vanished. Agnes chopped the brittle stems with a wooden guillotine, and combed them on iron spikes that resembled a medieval instrument of torture (and which she wielded as such) until the silky hairs glistened.

"Ready to spin for the long winter evenings when we sit with the women in the schoolhouse," I remarked. "Do you suppose the Tanito will read aloud for us from Petofi and Molnár Ferenc as he did last year?" Agnes glowered and said nothing.

At about this time, Kovacs had a heart-to-heart talk with Feri. His sister Etelka was about to marry and his mother was about to die. At last there was a real prospect of his being free to get married himself. "Etelka will need our furniture. I must marry a girl who will bring me something. You know this Maria of Torda? Her father rides behind his own horses, and not in a wagon either—a carriage! And he has ten cows, so would probably give her five."

"Isn't she that stupid-looking girl you were talking with last market day?" Feri asked. "I'd give you one week living with her, and you'd be ready to drive her home along with her five cows!"

A month later, Agnes and I were braiding a heap of onions to hang for winter. At first I thought the tears she brushed aside, like mine, came from the onions. Then she spoke. "Tiszteletes Asszony, the only thing left for me now, the only thing left for my life, would be to have someone who writes—writes books, I mean—tell about it."

Sobs were coming now, but when she was able to speak a few moments later, it was with a new objectivity, as if she saw her words dignified between the covers of a book. With epic slowness, Agnes continued. "He's not going to marry Maria. He's going to marry a girl from Aranyos Csucs. I thought for a while I'd either have to kill him or kill myself," she added tonelessly, ". . . a nice enough girl, poor thing, with a good dowry."

Gathering momentum, she told her story.

"When Kovacs Janos first came riding into Meszko on a bicycle, in his striped suit, 'That's the new Tanito,' they told me. The old teacher's wife was my friend, so it was I who gave him the six scrambled eggs for dinner." She tied the sixth onion, as though symbolically, into her wreath, and went on. "I dreamed he took me to Torda. Then I dreamed he kissed me. Yoy! I had no parents who read their child's face to see if there is trouble there."

"Is that why you came to work for me, to be near him?" I asked gently.

"He looked to me like a seventeen-story house! Did you think, Tiszteletes Asszony, that I came to your house, God forgive me, to help you? Did your husband think I went to church because I was religious? I went to church because Kovacs Janos played the organ. I felt as though the whole world were mine if only I got a glimpse of him. He's short and maybe ugly," Agnes granted. "But once when I was coming out of a cornfield, he was there on the road in front of me. When I pushed apart those corn leaves and saw him, 'Yoy!' I cried, 'Yoy!', just like that. When I saw he knew, every bit of strength left me."

"Do you think he'd marry you if you had a dowry?"

"If he would only think, he'd know I have something better than a dowry. I've got my strong back and my two hands. He's poor, and I know how to work. I'd know when there's this much bread," she said, carving off imaginary slices on one hand with the other. "I'd lift him up out of poverty."

"Then, of course, it had to be that there was a child—his and mine. If I couldn't be with him, at least I'd have that much of him," she mused.

I looked at Agnes with wonder. Was this woman, burdened all her years with a string of younger brothers and sisters, almost to the point of hating children, ready to be burdened again, with the additional odium of village mockery? Any hope on my part that Agnes would have the child, that I might help her, was all but dispelled by the flat bitterness of her voice.

"Kovacs said no. The child would bring him harm. The child would have to go."

"Oh, no. Why didn't you tell me?"

"Abortions are costly," Agnes responded. "I heard of a doctor in Kolozsvár. I went to see him. His fee was 2,000 lei."

Twelve American dollars! With a faint fling of hope, I asked, "But you didn't have that much money, did you?"

"Of course not. Kovacs wanted to be fair; he wanted to pay half. But he needed all his money just then because the Romanians were requiring all Magyar teachers to take a new examination in the Romanian language. He had to go away for several days to take it. I told the doctor we had no money and he said never mind, he could use some rabbits. Could I get him 2,000 lei worth of rabbits?"

"But there are no rabbits in Meszko!"

"There are no rabbits in the whole Aranyos Valley! Besides, I would have to go far away where people do not know me and would not ask, 'What does she want with rabbits?'"

Agnes had fabricated an errand to take her far from home. She borrowed the biggest basket she could find. Before the earliest Meszko wagons were on the road, she turned, not toward town but up into the mountains. After hiking fifteen kilometers of stony trail among steep, brush-covered hills, she came to the first cluster of Romanian houses.

"Have the Hungarians taken to eating rabbits?" asked a Romanian woman with surprise, as she lowered the first vigorously kicking rabbit under the lid of Agnes's basket.

As Agnes went from house to house, she found that rabbits were hard to pry loose from their owners. Meat was scarce, and those people raised barely enough for their own families. But her basket got heavier and harder to carry, since it was prone to the animals' lurches. Nor was her task made easier by the ever-present curiosity she encountered. "How come a Hungarian, and a girl at that, would bother to climb way up here into the Romanian world for rabbits?" she was asked. But Agnes knew enough Romanian to parry their questions and drive bargains.

After two days, the basket was loaded. Then she was faced with the problem of how to get it over many miles to Kolosvár. She dared not risk a ride over the public highway by wagon. The shortcut lay through her own village and across the precipitous gorge where Szent Laszlo had fled from the Cumans. To avoid being seen by her neighbors, she negotiated this difficult terrain by night. The downhill walk from the Romanian village, with the lively basket of rabbits on her head, was more difficult than uphill. By sunset, Agnes was on the outskirts of Meszko. She hid in the bushes until the village was safely asleep, then skirted it for the long walk in the dark, across the high prairie to the jagged drop into the gorge.

"I prayed to the good God that helped Szent Laszlo cross that ground to help me, too. The way to help me would have been to close up the split in the earth he'd made for the saint. But I was a sinner. Then I thought for a moment that maybe

God was with me, because the moon came out. But in the faint moonlight, rocks and shadows became confused. Yoy! *Istenem!*" Suddenly Agnes stumbled and the basket fell, its top jolting loose. In a flash, the rabbits were leaping in every direction.

"Did you get any back?"

"It was a nightmare. I'd grab for a rabbit and catch hold of a rock. I finally gave up. So I went back home and started all over again."

On her next attempt, Agnes had to climb to Romanian villages higher up and farther away. She did not try to cross the gorge again. She caught a ride with a Romanian wagon going to Kolosvár down the other side of the mountain. "How long did you stay at that doctor's?" I asked gently.

"A day and a night. Then I took a bus to Torda and walked home from there."

"Walked!" I cried. "But were you all right? Are you all right now?"

"My pain is in my soul," she answered.

After that, Agnes went to her old home to live and work. She did not want to come near the Papilak any more. Occasionally I would find her behind a mound of vegetables in the Torda market. "What's the matter, Agnes?" I asked one day at the market. "You're not well."

"I haven't eaten since yesterday morning," she admitted. "Tiszteletes Asszony, will you come where I can talk to you? I don't know what to do."

I took Agnes to Steppers, a cafe famous for its coffee and Viennese rolls. At a little table she told me about the widower of Rakas and his several nearly grown children. The widower had heard that Agnes was strong and capable, and he was interested in her.

"I went to visit them," she said. "The boys seemed orderly enough and would do as they were told, and the old grandmother said she'd be glad to have me come. The girl's eighteen; I don't know about her. But they need somebody. There are thirty acres and six oxen. What I really want is to get away from Meszko," she declared.

"What's he like?" I inquired.

"I don't know . . . not too *paraszt*, maybe. But he wants me to come now, when there's the most work, of course. He weeps and begs me to come. What do you think about a man who weeps?"

"Don't be rushed into it. Get to know him better," I responded.

Two weeks later I met Agnes on the street in Torda. She burst into tears. "He bought me stockings and a pair of shoes. I wore his ring. I said I'd marry him. But he didn't want to waste time coming to see me. I said I wasn't a cow to be driven home from market right away, like that. And he wouldn't put down in writing that I'd get an equal share with his children when he dies. Then he turned mean, and said if I didn't marry him at once, he'd sue my brothers for the shoes."

"They—my brothers—say I've disgraced our family for getting myself betrothed and breaking it off for no reason," she continued. "Last night they all got together and turned me out of the house. Me, to whom they owe everything they've ever had!"

"Where is your brother Pali now?"

"He's in town. I don't want to meet him. He says he's going to beat me because he's afraid that man will sue him."

"I don't believe he can sue," I snapped. "I'll try to find Pali."

First I hunted up a lawyer friend and got advice. Then I scoured the marketplace for Pali, who was brooding among the horses. I reported, "The lawyer says, 'Give the man back his ring, and that's all there is to it.' There's nothing to be ashamed of." Relieved, Pali and I together sought Agnes to give her the good news.

That was my last real encounter with my friend. I took seriously the commission Agnes laid upon me to solemnize in writing the tragedy of her life, as though there was no prospect of happiness, no promise for the future.

Decades later, I received a photograph of Agnes and the man she ultimately married. From the picture, I judged that her husband was a good man and not *parazst*. From the expression on her face it appeared that Agnes finally found satisfaction. On the back of the photo she had written, "With much love."

One More Time

Feri found an outlet for his frustrations through his prolific writing. In *A Stream of Stories*, a book of fables for all ages, he expressed his philosophy of education. He applied Jesus' life and work in the context of a typical Transylvanian village in *A Simple Gospel of Jesus*. In *Walk Around the World*, he shared his travel experiences and adventures. He wrote *Under the Clod*, a book about his successes and failures in Meszko. By the time it was published in 1936, Feri was seriously ill.

Feri had begun *Under the Clod* two years earlier, around the time of the Copenhagen conference and the trial. Too weak to do parish work after a severe bout of bronchitis, he sat in his chair and wrote, reflecting upon his efforts at village education and ideas about cooperating for community improvement. After he left for the conference, I wrote him in August of 1934, "Feri, my dear, I'm going to Torda to get shoes for Enika and have that horrid lump on her head looked at by Dr. Markovics. It is bigger than it was, and yesterday I noticed that the broken edges of the bone . . . seem to be drawing further apart.

"I hope you slept well last night! It was sweet to be near you and feel that in a measure the hardness of the past weeks has been dissolved. It can give us greater ground for faith. We love each other and can trust in it.

"I cannot just accept your arguments about there being no danger, though. I've been looking again at the *Britannica*: 'Man is liable to infection from two main sources: the first and infinitely more important being infected persons. The second, milk. Those suffering from the chronic type with cavities are perhaps the most dangerous of all. . . . Such persons establish the greatest concentration of infective matter within the home . . . adequate provision of hospital and sanatorium accommodation is also a prime necessity so that infected persons may be removed from amongst their still healthy relatives.'"

None of us was well that fall and winter. The nature and gravity of our ailments was at first unclear. Gradually we learned and only haltingly accepted that our universal family problem was tuberculosis.

On October 7, 1934, I wrote to Aunt Isabel, "Here is a free moment, when our cold supper of sheep's milk cheese, bread, milk, and tomatoes is on the table, and no Feri, so I'll 'improve' it by talking to you. It's a good feeling to sit down; the last days have been hectic.

"We have four Gypsies plastering our house. It had to be done, as the beams of the walls are thoroughly dried, and it no longer does any good to put mud between the cracks. The Morgans' $100 came in good time to keep us warm this winter. . . . The house is really charming, and when the garden grows as we plan it, the place will be beautiful.

"I'm keeping Enika in bed until it gets warmer, as her throat seems a bit husky. Last week she spent three days in bed with a mysterious temperature which I could trace neither to a cold, nor to her stomach, though she had no appetite. She's the most ticklish child about eating.

"Several days later: Today I went in to Torda by train, as they are conscripting horses in the valley and we don't want to exhibit our Jancsi. I had dinner with Mrs. Bagge, read and rested, then had afternoon tea and caught the four o'clock train to Szan Mihaly, laden with a big basket of grapes and pears and some cakes. I also had the basket of my own marketing, and it was quite a walk across the fields to Meszko.

"As I approached the bridge I saw a dark figure and a tiny white dancing one coming down the hill, and soon Enika came rushing toward me, laughing, and hugged my knees. She is so animated and intelligent and affectionate.

"If only I can see that she has health to carry it off! She ate well tonight: an egg, a whole bun brought from Torda, with a square inch of butter, a glass of milk, two pears, and a number of grapes. I have to make cooking for Enika the main business of my life. I shall be able to take better care of her, now I have a maid again. Your generous help of 100 Danish crowns every two months has allowed it. . . .

"I should be able to work things out so that I shall have time to write. In the last two weeks of spare moments, I have jotted down about 5,000 words. Just what it will be, I can't say. . . . Nevertheless, I'm at it, and feel that here is where happiness lies."

Although Christmas 1934 was a time of happy excitement, it was clouded by apprehension. In the morning, the bells of both the Romanian and Magyar churches chimed out together. If only it were symbolic of their human relations! On Christmas Eve, the Romanian *Kalindalok* or carolers were about. Indoors was Enika's little tree, realistic with white cotton snow, and fairylike with white candles, silver nuts, and bird-shaped cookies! Also, according to custom, a kind of Fourth of July sparklers. Presents were distributed by sweet Ilonka. Jula Neni did herself proud with Christmas dinner. The goose she had been fattening for weeks was transformed into soup with rice and vegetables, then roast goose with sour cabbage and plum sauce.

For about ten weeks I had been running a consistent temperature and had intermittent, stabbing pains in my chest, but not so strong as I remembered them to be in Berkeley when I had tubercular pleurisy. An x-ray showed some slight darkish spots in the middle of my lung.

For a month Enika and I were taken into the home of friends in Torda so I could have complete rest. When Feri was able to get Jula Neni to live with us, we returned to the village. After five weeks there was no change in temperature, so Mrs. Bagge drove me to Kolozsvár to the lung specialist who had examined me when I first came to Meszko. He said he neither heard nor saw anything new. Yet the continuous temperature and pricking pains were a sign of something. He told me to rest outdoors eight hours a day and gave me a prescription for some pills, Chinosol Peroval. As long as I took it, the fever disappeared, but the minute I stopped it came back just as before.

Feri had a much more serious condition. Worried, I wrote to Aunt Isabel, "Feri's intermittent temperatures and bronchitis have settled during the last five weeks to a steady pace. The cooperative doctor . . . thinks that Feri's bronchitis is of tuberculosis character. He cannot stand the least cold air; it brings a congested feeling in his lungs and sends his temperature up. We are going to the Kolozsvár specialist for a thorough examination.

"Four years ago when he was ill, the doctors thought there must be tubercular bacilli in his sputum, but they made two examinations and never found any. On the strength of this, Feri is pathetically confident that there can be none now. But of course I want this examined. Both the *Britannica* and my US government bulletins speak of the danger to children in living with tuberculosis parents. The cooperative doctor, however, thinks that the likelihood of establishing immunity counteracts any possible danger. Two opposing theories—which to believe?

"If the Kolozsvár specialist should advise it, there is a good, not too expensive sanatorium . . . where Feri might go. In that event, I suppose it would be best for Enika and me to stay here with Jula Neni and Ilonka and whoever will be the substitute minister.

"Before Feri was ill, my thoughts were turning to California. The specialist said that if there was no change in a month . . . I would do well to find a climate and general living conditions more favorable to recovery. . . . Feri was very much opposed to putting such a great distance between us, and then he became ill too!

"The ideal thing would be if both Feri and I come to America, rest and recover in a decent climate. . . . The trouble is that if we come it can only be for a year, as Unitarian ministers lose their church after a longer absence. Not that Meszko would be such a great loss, but if Feri steps out of his present village and tries for reappointment to another, he comes under the bishop's power. Bishop Boros would be delighted to have a chance not to reappoint him!

"Feri's book will in all probability be published in the spring. He can count on at least $150, probably $200, and about twice as much, if the book goes well in Hungary."

On January 3, 1935, I wrote again, "My temperature has come down in the last few days. But . . . the area in Feri's lungs has increased. . . . The Bagges have asked the Kolozsvár specialist to come to examine him here. He can advise whether he should go to a sanatorium. A Mr. Hankinson, an Englishman who calls himself a Unitarian-Quaker and works in Budapest, turned up unexpectedly and promised to get help if necessary for sanatorium expenses.

"Of course Feri would go alone, but it's a question whether such a journey is to be undertaken. It'll probably end by his staying right here and our investing in a brick stove . . . as it is no rest for him to get up four or five times at night renewing his fire in the little iron stove. Jula Neni, Ilonka, and Berta, a student minister, are still with us."

Early in the new year, things got worse. Feri had to go to a sanatorium because the risk was too great for both Enika and me. We were looking at a year-long separation. It probably would be another one to two years before Feri could take up his work again. Optimist that he was, Feri believed that he would recover in six months and come back to carry out the minimum requirements of a minister in Meszko.

My health was classified as borderline. The doctor said that I must be separated from Feri because a change of climate would be desirable for me, and advised me to return to California if it were possible. I was no source of danger to Enika, so we could be together.

I didn't know what to do. I thought of staying elsewhere in Transylvania, but it would not be the change of climate the doctor advocated. The trouble with traveling as far as California was that the journey would take all my money, leaving me very little to live on. I considered Palestine because it was nearby and I would be able to come back in case of a crisis with Feri. But the doctor assured me that he anticipated nothing of this sort and said Feri's recovery was just a matter of time. Feri had always been unwilling to consider for a moment my going to America, but after the doctor talked to him, he was willing and acquiescent. He was a model patient and cheerfully anticipated the time when he could write in bed.

On February 1, 1935, I wrote to Aunt Isabel, "Feri is now in the State Hospital in Kolozsvár . . . till spring, when he hopes to be well enough to live in the little house out on the hill. . . . I am still with Enika and Ilonka in the room in Torda, but expect to go out to Meszko as soon as I hear that Luci, the girl theological student, can come to spend February with us. I shall continue to rest out of doors.

"Of course nothing would make me happier than if we all could come to America. . . . I can decide nothing about the future, however, until I know better how Feri is. I can see that the thought of my going so far away and for so long depresses him terribly, and I don't want to do anything which might be a retarding influence on his health. On the other hand, I'm not going to be inveighed into living with Enika under the same roof with him until there is every assurance of no danger of contagion.

"Next winter will be a test. . . . It may be that he can never live in a winter climate again. If so, then we'll have to take steps toward living in America. He wanted to fix up the third room in our house, which is well separated, to live in, with Enika and me in the other two rooms. I wouldn't hear of it. . . . The risk of indirect contact is too great.

"If I try to come to America, I'll have to go to Bucharest about my passport. I can come on my American, but I may get into snarls with the Romanians about a separate Romanian pass for Enika. . . . Then I'll probably have to renounce my Romanian citizenship and pay up all the back taxes as a foreigner living in this country all these years. I could come on my Romanian passport, but that would mean running the gauntlet of Ellis Island, and if I developed a conspicuous temperature they'd ship me back."

Enika continued to be my emotional mainstay, a distraction from Feri's illness, and my eternal hope, even though her fragile health was always a source of worry. Being ill, it concerned me that so many "outsiders" were having a hand in her daily life.

Early in 1935, Enika and I moved back to Meszko. Feeling stronger, I decided to stay on for the whole summer. If we were to eat the next winter I didn't see how I could leave our garden. Despite the uncertainty of the years ahead, I had planted fruit trees, Isabella grapes, roses, and a lawn. If I went away for the summer they would be stolen or neglected. I loved the garden that year as never before.

On March 28, 1935, I went to visit Feri in Kolozsvár. He had been in considerable pain and asked the doctor if the injections he'd been receiving were responsible. For a week the doctor answered "No." Then as the pain increased, he admitted that sometimes there was this reaction. I didn't know what they would decide to do next. I was feeling much better, but worried about Enika. After a bout with the flu, her fever hung on for six weeks. I was advised to let her run about in the spring sunshine.

In April, I received another letter from Mrs. Morgan with virtually a job offer for Feri under the Tennessee Valley Authority. Feri would not hear a word. He was dead set on giving life here two or three more years' trial. If I said how splendid is the work of the TVA, he replied that what he was trying to do in Meszko was splendid, too.

Of course I was free to leave this country (barring possible troubles with passports) whenever I pleased. Feri's "not letting" me meant that he was convinced beyond persuasion that if I went away (America or Denmark), he would not recover. He made me feel responsible for his life, so what could I do but stay? The situation was the same as the two other times he was ill. The thought that I was so far away and might possibly never come back, in spite of assurances from me to the contrary, made him so depressed that it affected his health.

Enika continued to run high temperatures so I took her to Kolozsvár to be x-rayed. The doctor said Enika probably had a little TB in her glands, that she was apparently very sensitive and must not be exposed to Feri as long as there was danger to her from him. I was advised to protect her from colds and grippe and to avoid contact with anyone who had a cold. When I told him our situation, he said that without a doubt it would be best for both of us to go to California. In the afternoon we went to Feri's doctor, Dr. Pap Livius, for an x-ray, which showed a darkening in the glands. He thought he saw a tiny spot in one lung, and also said we should go to California.

During the morning in Kolozsvár, I had taken Enika to see Feri at the sanatorium. He came out on the porch and talked to us across the railing. I had not told Enika we were going to see him, so it was a tremendous surprise. She heard his voice first from indoors and called to him. When he appeared, she said in Hungarian, "Here is your little girl!"

Feri dressed and came out to sit on a bench in the sun for a few minutes. When I tried to keep Enika from touching him, he became very angry and said there was a limit to such American precautions. I replied that a Transylvanian doctor that very morning had advised us against touching him or his things. Feri was absolutely blind and wouldn't listen to me. It was the same fury he always had when I tried to protect Enika from people who had a cold. He said he would not come home this summer if I was going to be so silly; that I would spoil our happiness and lives by such precaution. I replied that such care could be taken quietly and sensibly, that it was his wild unreasonableness that spoiled things, and that if he was going to persist in such an attitude he had better not come back to Meszko.

While we were with Dr. Livius in the afternoon, Feri surprised us by coming down from the sanatorium. He was in a less hard mood, probably partly to make up for the way he had spoken in the morning. He said now that he seemed to be getting better he "would allow" us to go. I felt, nonetheless, that his inner attitudes were unchanged, that he would be broodingly angry, bitter, and unhappy if we went away. Before, he had said my going away would be the end of our marriage. If I went it should be with the understanding that he would not follow. He seemed to look upon it merely as the assertion of my desire for my own country and work pitted against his. With Feri, a man's work and plans came first, and the woman made the adaptations. Even though that was what I'd been trying to do for four years!

"Feri is probably coming home to live up in The Little House next week," I wrote to Aunt Isabel. "There are some difficult months ahead. I shall wait to see how Feri and Enika both fare. It may be that Feri's impossible state of mind is a sign of acute illness and I don't want, if I can help it, to inflict the blow of our departure.

"Enika's temperature is slight now. . . . Enika has an intense will and a temper when crossed. Of course I have faith in her native sweetness, intelligence, and humor, but she's a little barbarian, and I hesitate to bring her into your very orderly and serene lives."

Five days after our argument in Kolozsvár, Feri had a hemorrhage and sudden rise of temperature. We talked only for a few minutes. He agreed to my going to California with Enika. He realized that husbands and wives do not always have a quieting effect on one another. We had to speak of very difficult things and he finally saw that while he was ill, it was better for us to be apart.

The doctors said the hemorrhage was not dangerous, that his recovery was well begun and that they had the best hope for him. He had not been getting proper food, so I arranged for food to be brought in to him from a good vegetarian restaurant.

On June 20, 1935, Feri's condition improved enough for him to come back to Meszko for a month's trial. The last x-ray showed that half the diseased area had cleared, but he still tested positive for tuberculosis. I had prepared The Little House for his stay, which was up the hill from our house, and hired a little girl to carry him food and water.

Enika had been running another temperature, which we thought was due to a touch of tuberculosis, but we found swelling in her head from an infected bone. Luckily, it was not near the brain.

When I saw Feri that June, I had second thoughts about my leaving. It would be such a long separation and possibly worsen the growing misunderstanding between us. But it seemed the only thing to do. For us and an assistant minister to live together next winter in a house that may not have been free from drafts promised too many difficulties.

"If only there were not such drawbacks, we would be a happy-enough family," I wrote to Aunt Isabel. "I have never been disappointed in the qualities which made me love Feri in the first place. He is still something of a hero to me. But one can sometimes be too heroic. Heroism is all right, maybe, if it is a clear alternative between great achievement and quick death. But if it entails a risk of a dragging illness, with trouble and expense to other people and involving a child's health, I say better choose the safe course, even if it costs dearly."

Anxiety hung as a cloud over those beautiful days of late spring, with new grass coming up and my new fruit trees putting forth leaves and a blossom or two. Finally Feri agreed to a possible sojourn in America. Then, he had second thoughts.

On July 20, 1935, I wrote to Aunt Isabel in frustration, "You'll need to take our plans with a grain of salt. . . . No sooner than Feri seemed final in his idea [of coming to] America . . . he began planning for the future here. He wants to try for a professorship in the Unitarian College in Kolozsvár. As an old professor may die or resign within the next two to four years, Feri thinks it best to stay here to be on deck for his chance. . . . As one of the professors remarked, in three years Feri's chief opposition may be 'in heaven.' In the meantime, he must write and make himself known. . . . Well, goodbye to my secret hope that Feri might get so interested in work in the TVA, we could live there always! Feri's sputum is still 'active' and his temperature averages 37 [100°F]. We probably should not live in the same house next fall. For me to spend all that money to come to America with the knowledge that Feri isn't coming, and that in a year I'd have to return to Transylvania, might be harder than not coming at all. But I'm going ahead with our passports anyway."

After the trial visit, the doctor advised Feri to spend the winter in a sanatorium, with the hope of returning to the village in spring. In early August, Count Banffy, once Foreign Minister of Hungary and a member of *Helicon*, promised to get a free place in one of the best Budapest sanatoriums for Feri. I didn't know what to do, travel to Berkeley or try to stay on in Budapest near Feri. His condition had neither improved nor worsened.

The lump on Enika's head seemed to be getting smaller, but within the last two months she had high temperatures. I didn't want her to have another winter like the last. Much depended on the living arrangements I could make in Budapest.

The bright spot of the late summer was that Feri's writing was getting recognition in Torda and Budapest, and promising a little income. A publishing house inquired about his book *Walk Around the World*. One of our darkest moments was when we learned that the infection on Enika's head was indeed tuberculosis.

On August 20, 1935, I wrote to Aunt Isabel, "These stupid doctors don't tell one the truth, on the supposition that the less one knows the better. I need your help. This past year has been nervewracking and difficult. Enika does not eat well and isn't the sweet-tempered baby she was; but with patience, firmness, and good environment I know she will be all right again." But the doctors assured us that Enika's condition was not serious. They said she did not need to rest, but should be outdoors as much as possible.

At the end of the summer Feri left for Budapest; a tired, forlorn figure. We took him by cow cart to the station. I dreaded to think of his long, all-night journey sitting up on the train. But he had to go, as he was getting no better in Meszko. I remained in the village to wait for Enika's passport.

Feri ended up going to Debrecen sanatorium, near Budapest. His illness was more serious than he knew and he finally realized that he had to give up Meszko.

Still he believed that he could come out of the sanatorium in about six months and after a few months of rest, be ready for some kind of work.

The head doctor at Debrecen wrote me that Feri could never get completely well. At best, he might better his circumstances, and for this, "long years" would be necessary. Although Feri's life was not in danger, the time had been too short for the doctor to say much more than that such cases could give great surprise, either in the direction of recovery or the opposite.

Suddenly came a report of a steadily lowering temperature from Feri. That good news, the assurance of the Kolozsvár doctors that he would get better, and his previous improvement in the Kolozsvár sanatorium, persuaded me toward America. Enika would get well more quickly, and I could get work in California or Colorado and create a place for Feri when he was well enough for the journey; probably in two years. The Torda doctor had said that it would not be safe for us to live together again for a minimum of two years.

By November, Enika and I were out of Romania and on our way to Denmark. The struggle I had getting Feri and Enika's passports was unimaginable, requiring constant journeying to innumerable offices. After three months of waiting, word came from Bucharest that they had received neither the money nor the birth certificate I had personally placed in the hands of the prefect in Torda. I had said to the prefect's secretary, "That I have such trouble getting a passport for a baby whose health depends upon it is a matter of shame to this country."

The secretary became angry. "Don't talk like that about this country or I'll do everything in my power to prevent your getting out!"

I was really worried then. When I told Mr. Bagge about it, he telegraphed his lawyer in Bucharest to get the passport there, if possible, and send it directly to the Danish consulate. It looked as though I might have to spend the winter in Torda. When at last the passport came, I had to pay twice for it.

During our journey out of Romania, the only difficulty had been at the Romanian frontier at midnight. While in Torda the prefect had said my documents were in order, at the frontier they said I had to pay a 1,000 lei fine. When I told them I had only 500, they threatened to take me off the train and bring me before court the next day. I wept, partly from genuine nervousness and partly to let them believe that they would have an hysterical female to deal with if they carried it too far. I rushed through the train trying to find someone who would loan me the extra 500 until Budapest, but no luck. Then at the very last second, the police returned my passports, pocketing the 500 lei. I had lied; I had just enough small change for a taxi in Budapest.

In our train compartment was a little German girl, and although she and Enika had no language in common, it made no difference. They played hilariously until after midnight. Once across the frontier, the little girl's mother and I set about the difficult job of tucking our children down to sleep. Enika was singing softly to herself when suddenly the woman sat bolt upright and directed a loud and awful "Pssst" at Enika in the dark.

Thoroughly startled, Enika came creeping over to me and whispered, "Mummy, let us pray!" This struck me as so funny that I began to laugh, and a great wave of relief at being out of Romania came over me.

We spent three days in Budapest. My Aunt Isabel had written, advising me to stay in Denmark. Feri added his approval to it, only instead of Denmark he thought I could put Enika in a children's sanatorium in Budapest or Austria, with Mr. Hankinson's money he was not using plus Isabel's monthly help. But his calculations were too optimistic. Such sanatoria were more expensive than he thought, and there would have remained nothing for me to live on. Mr. Hankinson called and told us that after six months Feri probably would have to pay his own way in the sanatorium, so we needed to save money for him. That left no choice but for Enika and I to go on to Denmark.

Feri had a high temperature again. They gave him a private room so he could regulate the air. I did not visit him at Debrecen, though I longed to. I was afraid that a visit from me would do more harm than good. He had written me earlier that he was all calm and peaceful, and that it would be easier if he had no association with me at Debrecen. I moved on to Prague and stayed one night with Dr. and Mrs. Norbert Capek. Dr. Capek said I was lucky to be getting out of south and central Europe, that general restlessness was increasing and German armaments were becoming more of a threat.

When we arrived in Denmark at my Uncle Otto's home, it was so gray and foggy, I was able to persuade Enika that it was still night. She went straight to bed and slept until noon. I wrote to Aunt Isabel, "It does seem that as soon as I hear that Feri is definitely improving, I should come to America and lay the foundations both for Enika's health and a future. Right now I am living with Uncle Otto and [cousin] Karen. . . . If [Enika] should get worse in this climate, it might be difficult to have her admitted to the United States."

I was torn between Feri and Enika; what was good for the one was not good for the other. Aunt Isabel suggested that I leave Enika in Denmark if Feri should get worse and want me near him. But I couldn't leave her with Karen, who had all she could do to take care of Uncle Otto. I doubted whether I could leave her with cousin Emmy Louisa either, since she had her hands full, too.

I received an affectionate and pathetic letter from Feri, in which for the first time, he urged America as the best place for Enika and me. He was getting worse, and he knew we had to plan in terms of years.

Early in December, the American consulate in Denmark nearly extinguished all hope. If Feri could never be completely cured, they seemed to insist, then he could never be admitted to the United States, even as a visitor. Anyone with tuberculosis, even if not "active," would not be allowed to enter the country.

Enika was tested for tuberculosis and the results were negative. Every day we walked by the sea, which fascinated her. She would ask, "Where do the ships spend the night? Where do they go when it rains?" She loved to feed the ducks in Oregaard's Park, and was indignant when one managed to grab more than his fellows. She saw some deer hanging outside a meat market and said, "Poor little fellows, were they killed? What for?" and when we ate chicken she often asked, "Did they kill it? With a knife?" I thought of asking Feri whether he had already indoctrinated her in the direction of vegetarianism.

I wrote to my father, "Feri seems to be in good spirits. He says that when his temperature is down in the evening, he reads and writes. A friend brings him all the books he wants from the big university library at Debrecen. . . . If he could stand the climate, I wonder if he would be content to live in Budapest. I'd prefer it to the poverty and cultural barrenness of a peasant village in Transylvania!

"However, in Hungary . . . democracy of any kind is nonexistent. Advancement or advantage goes by *protekcio* (pull). If I were in Romania now I could be put in prison for having written this to you. So much the quicker, if these remarks were publicly printed, because there is even a law that anyone saying anything, true or not, which is critical of the country is guilty of crime. There are things I'd like to write, but Feri asks me not to, as it might make serious trouble for him if ever he wants to live there again. . . .

"I feel that I have changed. I am somewhat of an unknown quantity to myself; so many old convictions and strong feelings have weakened. I don't know where I'll be or what I'll do, what I am capable of doing or what openings there will be."

In Denmark, I had an opportunity to teach at the International College. I had a class of advanced students in English—there were Norwegians, Swedes, Danes, and one Finn. They were quick and able to carry on discussions, and I was glad to see their shyness and stiffness gradually break away. I was experiencing a revival of mind and spirit. It was good to be in a free country again.

For two months I taught and attended an occasional class. Feri was growing impatient in the sanatorium and talked of coming out to be at his mother's. The Denmark consul was flat and final to the impossibility of getting him into the United States while he had tuberculosis. Feri thought I should come to Debrecen to nurse him or at least be near him. He thought I should put him first and Enika second, but I couldn't see it that way. I could not risk having Enika under the same roof with Feri, or with me if I was to be in fairly continuous contact with him. He was positively bitter about it. I didn't know how it would all end.

In June of 1936, I received unexpected news. Feri had left Debrecen and returned to Meszko. The doctors thought his case hopeless. This may be the last year of his life, I thought. His book about his village experiences, *Under the Clod*, had been published. "Criticisms are favorable," he had written, "one of them even saying it is the outstanding Hungarian book of this generation!" If I returned to Romania, I could translate it into English, with his help. It would give him something to think about and not be too strenuous for him.

By the end of July I was still in Denmark. Contrary to the doctor's expectation, Feri was better, due to the warm weather, which made it imperative that he get south that winter. If he was really on the upgrade and it wasn't necessary for me to go south with him, I intended to go to America and take whatever work I could get.

In October, events took a swift and surprising turn. Through the efforts of Mr. Morgan, US Secretary of State Cordell Hull created an opening for all three of us to make the journey to America. The Secretary granted special permission for Feri to come if he would directly enter a United States sanatorium. Out of a sense of urgency, I sent Enika on ahead to stay with my cousin Catherine in California. It was an unorthodox and intuitive move on my part, and perhaps highly risky, putting four-year-old Enika in the hands of a near stranger for the voyage to America. But since

Enika needed to leave immediately, I felt I hardly had a choice. Fate provided opportunity and a safe passage. Her companion was a young man from the International People's College, who offered to take her with him from Liverpool to New York. When Enika's boat stopped in Ireland, the young man wrote me a note, reassuring me that she was having a good trip. She had played happily and enjoyed a party that the boat had arranged for all the children.

After seeing Enika off, the plan was for me to wait in London for word that Feri was on his way to Berlin, where we were to meet. We would sail together to America from Bremen. Then, on our arrival in New York, word would be waiting for us as to whether we were to go to Florida or Tennessee.

However, instead of sailing to America, I returned to Romania. While waiting in Meszko for his passport, Feri's condition had worsened. He had been taken to a hospital in Torda and told that I probably would not return.

When I saw him alone in his tiny bed in that vast, empty space, I was shocked. He had been placed in what resembled a desolate, lonely barracks. He was hardly able to talk because he was so depressed. Afterwards, I went back to the hotel and cried my heart out as I had never cried before.

The next day I had him moved into a more pleasant room, which lifted his spirits. I soon found a small apartment for us in Torda and a small teaching job. Dear Jula Neni, bless her, came to help. As there was no extra bed, she slept on the kitchen table. In those supportive surroundings, Feri recovered his spirits and wrote about his religious philosophy in an essay entitled, "Religion for the New Man." He also worked on a novel, *Green Flood*, in which he described his struggle.

By November 21, Feri still had no passport. We were told that all his documents were lost. If things went smoothly, it would take another five or six weeks to get another passport. Enika's journey had gone off well. Catherine wrote that Enika spoke English fluently, and that they loved having her. Feri was miserably thin, without much appetite, and had a daily temperature. He was beginning to give up on coming to America. I hoped he didn't.

In December Feri was critically ill. He was very weak and practically reduced to a skeleton. He was in fair spirits, however, and full of plans for writing. I longed to see Enika, but I could not leave Feri.

Christmas arrived with gifts from Aunt Isabel. My class had decreased from thirteen to two pupils. For no apparent reason, I was ordered by the Romanian government to leave the country within forty-eight hours, but was saved temporarily by the influence of Romanian friends of friends. I sent an appeal to Bucharest, knowing that if they put me out, they would probably never let me in again.

By April of 1937, it did not look as if Feri would pull through. I thought he had survived the worst of winter, but he came down with influenza. He wasn't in much pain, but the coughing became extremely difficult and he was very weak. He was such a courageous person. Only now did he suspect that he might not live long, and arranged his writings and things in a very matter-of-fact way.

When spring came, Feri seemed better in appetite and spirits, but the high temperature was even higher. He liked to be read to and to listen to symphonies over the radio from Budapest. Although he was not in pain, he suffered most from extreme weakness and the fatigue of coughing. I wrote to my stepmother, "It *is* a tragedy that he must die so young. People here and in Hungary feel it, because he was a genuine leader. But as Mr. Morgan says about him in his little book, *The Long Road*, 'He couldn't run a mile, but might have walked ten.' If only he could have gone slower and not tried to do the work of a dozen men.

"The nursery school in Claremont wrote a splendid report of Enika—her independence, imagination, and sweet way of dealing with children littler than herself. Isn't life, as the Hungarians say, *finom vegyes*, a fine mixture, happiness and sorrow so closely and intricately bound together?"

On May 21, the day was especially lovely. Feri seemed so quiet and peaceful. He smiled several times and enjoyed being talked and read to. He was awake more than usual, so I was with him more. He seemed so well, in fact, that the doctor said he might live another three months.

In a few hours, he had difficulty breathing. I called the doctor at ten in the evening. He gave Feri a morphine injection, telling him it was something to strengthen his heart, and told him to sleep. Although he tried dutifully, Feri opened his eyes and said like a willful child, "I'm not going to sleep."

I said, "You don't have to sleep just because someone tells you to," and he smiled roguishly, as I hoped he would.

Soon he did sleep, and half woke for a few seconds off and on until dawn, when the struggle for air began again. The doctor lived nearby and soon was there with more morphine, but not enough. The following half hour seemed unnecessarily difficult and Feri never lost consciousness. He said he wanted to spit, and struggled to sit up. I helped him, but it was no use. In a moment he sank back and it was over.

Ceremonies of Life and Death

For the most part, village funerals and weddings were patterns of pageantry set against a background of nature. Once when I sat in Jula Neni's yard, her baby goats leaping in and out of my lap, a Romanian funeral procession came up the road. As was the custom, the black gilded banners with their swinging loaves of bread came to a halt where two roads intersect to make a cross. The processioners sang and prayed and then moved along. First were the standard bearers in white linen and lace surplices, then the chanting cantor, the bearers of the white lace-covered coffin, and the new young minister in his skirts and bowler hat. He bowed remotely to me.

Then followed the crowd of women: black silhouettes of bell-shaped petticoats; faces of tragic, pale ovals under black kerchiefs knotted under their chins. There was our Romanian postman, our Romanian neighbor Gavrila, and other familiar faces now suddenly strange and set apart. Those somber human beings seemed an intrusion upon the green and flowering spring landscape. When they passed, my eyes returned gladly to our little circle of tumbling children, dancing goats, and Jula Neni crouching over her onion bed.

Perhaps to offset a life of toil, almost any appeal to the emotions was welcomed by the villagers. Sometimes expression of feeling at funerals appeared to be sheer dramatics, and would reach its height after the service in the church when the coffin was carried up the hill to the cemetery. It was then that members of the family cried aloud their personal recollections of the deceased. "Yoy, Jani, you bought me a pair of shoes. You gave me money for a new dress!"

In contrast was the burial of another young man, one of the serious members of Feri's folk school group. Bensze Miklos and his mother had taken one of our lands, the "bull's place," for a share of the crop. After a morning cultivating corn, a sudden thunderstorm arose. Miklos and his mother took shelter beneath a large oak on the edge of the field. But the tree was struck by lightning. When the mother came to, she found her son lying prostrate. She shook and called him in vain. Trying to rise, she found her lower body paralyzed. On hands and knees, the mother dragged herself up and down the hills for five miles back to Meszko, to get help for her son.

I saw her after the men returned to tell her that Miklos was dead. She sat immobile, save for a stately rocking rhythm. Her face under the black kerchief was transfixed with grief, but with the expression of almost a smile such as one sees in Giotto's paintings of mourning women. "My soul, my star!" she kept saying, "the one upon whom our whole family depended." During the three days that followed, she possessed the dignity of a figure in a Greek tragedy. She was being herself but at the same time playing a part, unself-consciously, almost impersonally, in the drama of life and fate.

Death was almost the only occasion when the Romanian and Hungarian communities forgot their differences and joined freely in one another's festivals. Gavrila was found fallen on his face in the snow, ax in one hand, newly cut tree in the other. All night his family sat beside the coffin. Next morning the neighbors baked funeral cakes. In the afternoon, our friend, the tall Greek Catholic priest, stood bareheaded before the coffin as it lay in the courtyard, his frayed velvet gown embroidered in tarnished silver, the glass-jeweled cross in his hand, the shabby banners with their dim and crackled paintings, and the little bare-branched tree hung with wrinkly winter apples cut in half, walnuts, biscuits, and a bright pink-frosted cake from the Torda market.

All contrasted startlingly with the plain, black-shawled crowd, Gavrila's crooked, straw-roofed house, his rough wooden implements, and the muddy courtyard with its bedraggled ducks and frightened hens. The little courtyard no longer bore the burden of the dead Gavrila. The priestly chant had lifted him into the mighty procession of the dead. One by one, members of his family came to place their hands on the coffin, a sign of mutual forgiveness of trespasses. The little tree was lifted up and down with all its apples and cakes swinging to the prayer that there might be sweets for Gavrila in the other world too. As snow was falling, the coffin was lifted up, and pure human grief was allowed to break forth once more from the black crowd.

I, too, wished Godspeed to my little monkey-like neighbor Gavrila, who always used to come out to smile and talk Romanian with Enika when we went past his gate.

By contrast, weddings reflected the mood of springtime. I was taken by surprise the first time two pretty Romanian girls jauntily walked into my kitchen, their crisp white aprons arching over ballooning, accordian-pleated skirts. One of them carried a huge bunch of flowers, the other a few flowers against something that looked like a round, white sofa pillow with trailing lace petticoats. Both wore coquettish sprigs on their bosoms and in their hair. The oldest gasped shyly, then launched into a long speech in Romanian, something very formal and impressive. I called on Agnes to translate: I had been invited to a Romanian wedding the next Sunday.

An hour later, two young Romanian men in shiny black boots appeared at our door. Against their black hats were gay evergreen wreaths with a red tissue paper rose in the center, and another rose in their lapels. Each flourished a cane wound in red and white tissue paper stripes, with long streamers. One of them carried a white cloth by its four corners, heavy with I knew not what. Once again, I was invited to the wedding.

"Quick, give them an egg!" whispered Agnes. I added my egg to the hundred others in the white cloth. "The bride will sell them and buy something for her new home," she explained.

Hungarian and Romanian weddings were much alike. Relatives and friends crowded the tiny house of the bride's parents and overflowed into the courtyard. Wine and *kalacs*, a white holiday bread, were passed around. Silence fell as the minister arrived and performed the ceremony. Then Gypsy musicians struck up their violins and helped the guests endure the wait for the feast to come. To prepare for the feast, plank tables were set up in a room cleared of all furniture. Black-skirted Nenis rushed to and fro, laying out the thick white china. Presently appeared the delicious duck soup with rings of golden fat concealing tangles of homemade noodles. Followed fried duck and chicken with rice and *ugorka*—cucumber pickle. Then every housewife untied a white napkin and set her donation of cake upon the table. There were a dozen varieties, and each guest was supposed to take home at least a taste of each.

Finally the most eloquent among the men rose and flung his hat upon the table, crying out: "Who is going to help this worthy young couple as they set forth together upon the long road of marriage? Everyone be generous! Remember how it was when you were young. I'll begin with 500 lei. Who's next?"

The Gypsies meanwhile, having had their fill in the kitchen, settled their violins under their chins. If it were a Romanian wedding, everyone took a few twirls with the bride. At home, toward dawn, I could still hear the Gypsy music, now disjointed and out of tune, serenading the streets of Meszko.

Szerelem was a special word for erotic love. Szerelem wove in and out of women's gossip on long winter evenings and in boys' talk as they came to sit with girls while they spun. A pretty face or a nice voice in the church choir, however, would not get a man far in the labor of living, unless they were accompanied by a strong back, a full hope chest, a strip of land, or a pair of oxen. So insisted the wisdom of age, for the parents, after all, had the final say in decisions of the heart. More so with a son than a daughter; a young woman could pack up her towels and tablecloths and run away with her beloved if he had a home to offer, while a man was dependent upon his parents' house and land. Young people often took matters into their own hands. Marriages often followed the conception of a child. On the other hand, I knew of several cases in Meszko where the parents' wills prevailed, pregnancy notwithstanding. Like almost everywhere else in the world, relations beween men and women were varied and complex.

Jula Neni's Ilonka became bonny and marriageable as I was leaving the country. She had nothing but her health, a lovely face, and a few fruit trees. A mischievous-faced boy, one of my favorites, who had quite a tract of land lying just next to Ilonka's, began to pay shy courtship to her.

"Yoy!" said Jula Neni in mock dismay, "everywhere I look, there is that boy! If they are not talking over this fence, it is over that one."

When I finally left Meszko, it made me happy to leave Ilonka all my household goods, in the hope that when the boy returned in two years from military service his parents would consider it enough for a proper dowry.

Late every fall, the Magyar villages look forward to the *Vilagitas* or "Lighting Up," an ancient, simple custom of remembrance of those who have died. The last fall I was in Meszko, I climbed with Jula Neni and others after dark up the hill to the Hungarian cemetery. Not knowing what to expect, I went with some hesitation.

As we went higher and higher up the hill and could overlook the valley, all the other villages near and far were distinguishable by large areas of hazy light. Torda's must have been several acres. The woods of our own hilltop were aglow under a radiant cloud of smoke from the candles. Thousands and thousands of candles were burning; every grave was like a huge rectangular birthday cake. White, pink, and deep red chrysanthemums, the flower that survives the bitter cold of late October, were everywhere in great bouquets, enormous wreaths, or growing, or stuck in the ground, according to pattern.

The scent of all those candles burning in beds of chrysanthemum was delicious, like that of old-time lighted Christmas trees. The candlelight touched the underside of the branches, making a vast arcade in which groups of black-kerchiefed women and red-aproned, red-kerchiefed girls, moved quietly among the columns of tree trunks, bending with lighted candles to remember a relative or friend. Children scurried about like rabbits, excited at being allowed to light candles and entranced by the fairylike spectacle. As I moved from group to group, I experienced many shades of moods. If there was weeping, it was silent or subdued. The self-conscious prominence of the funeral and the protestations of personal grief gave way to a larger feeling of community and acceptance.

Feri's body had been laid to rest in the Hungarian cemetery in Meszko. A simple, beautifully carved wooden marker carried the inscription: "Balázs Ferenc, Minister, 1901-37." I liked to think that Jula Neni would bring chrysanthemums and candles to his grave, and that villagers would remember his hopes for them again each year at Vilagitas.

During the years following my return to America in 1937, through the period of World War II, I heard only once from Transylvania. Feri had looked upon his final illness as the chance to write about our successes and failures in Meszko. Because it was such an honest account, *Under the Clod* was adopted by Hungarian young people as a guide to the future. For a time at least, it was regarded as a Transylvanian classic. During the days when Hungary was slipping under the vise-like control of Hitler, the book was widely circulated as an opposing, democratic influence. Feri's novel, *Green Flood*, had success in Hungary as well.

Later I learned that during the war Meszko had been bombed, and that our little church and minister's house were partly destroyed. The cooperatives in the valley and their central outlet in Torda survived, however. Some years after his death, Feri's sister in Budapest wrote to me that a people's college, named for Feri and patterned after his ideas, had been established in Hungary.

Feri's was a beautiful life ended too soon because his will, imagination, and activity were too strong for one slight body. During the last few years of his life, he lived more intensely and accomplished more than many average lives rolled into one. He was a great man among the Transylvanian-Hungarians.

Were we happy together? I think we had greater happiness and greater unhappiness than is the lot of most people. I was with him in his work and ideals, but I could not save him from overactivity and a too-determined will.

He misunderstood my desire to get him to America for his health's sake as mere desire to leave Transylvania. I knew he could never get well there, and he never would realize the seriousness of his illness, nor the need to guard Enika.

I am glad I was with him for those last seven months. It was not an easy time, for he did not want to recognize any danger to those around him, and bitterly resented ordinary precaution. I kept hoping he would get sufficiently well to live quietly and write. I had the feeling that if we could have come through this time and had a few more years together, we would have come to a deep and perfect understanding.

Vilagitas

I want everyone to know
that I did not die here.
My village's moods and problems
did not drown me.
I sowed myself only into
this tiny place.
I hid myself all over here
under the clod.
Let me be seen thus:
I will sprout in these fields
in the spring.
There will be blossoms here
which will bear good fruit.
—Francis Balázs

Feri Balazs
1901-1937

Christine Morgan
1903-1996

Notes

American Unitarian Association

"The armistice in 1918 released the denomination's creative potential for reconstruction abroad and growth at home. Many Unitarians supported President Wilson's struggle for a League of Nations and his campaign for American ratification. . . .

"The mistreatment of religious minorities in eastern Europe touched a raw nerve. The problem centered in Transylvania, the ancient Carpathian kingdom where Unitarianism had first emerged to history in the mid-sixteenth century. Under the Treaty of Versailles, Transylvania, historically a province of Hungary, was ceded to Romania. The Romanian government proceeded to deny basic liberties to the Transylvanians, regarding the country, according to one account, as a 'conquered territory.' Confiscation of schools and churches, commandeering of dwellings, restrictions on the rights of public worship and public assembly were widespread. A series of visitations, chiefly from English and American Unitarians, and the formation of an English and later an American Committee on Religious Rights and Minorities, served to call the world's attention to the conditions in Transylvania, and, in the words of one AUA officer, helped to 'stay the hand of ruthlessness and to give these minority institutions a better fighting chance for functioning and for surviving.'

"But with the advent of the Great Depression in 1929, many Unitarian churches lost heavily in the stock market. The AUA's income from investments plummeted, forcing heavy cutbacks in salaries, travel, and aid to churches. As the AUA's state of depression deepened, churches closed and growing numbers of ministers became unemployed or were forced to take second jobs."

By 1934, the world was still recoiling from the depression and Adolf Hitler had been in power for a year. "Unitarian churches were in sharp decline, and some people even feared that Unitarianism might die as an institution. Dr. Louis C. Cornish, president of the American Unitarian Association, painted a dismal picture of the situation [in his annual report for 1934]: 'Churches are being consolidated; churches are being closed. One Protestant denomination reports 500 unemployed ministers in New England alone. There is no need of amplifying these statements. There is need to remember that the present day conditions affect every cooperative endeavor, including the work of the American Unitarian Association. It has been impossible for this Association to do all we would wish it to do.'"

—Excerpted and adapted from "A Wave at Crest" by David B. Parke and "It Was Noontime Here ..." by Carol R. Morris in *A Stream of Light: A Short History of American Unitarianism*, edited by Conrad Wright (Boston, Massachusetts: Skinner House Books, 1989)

Cooperatives

"An organization owned by and operated for the benefit of those using its services. Cooperatives have been successful in a number of fields, including the processing and marketing of farm products. . . . The income from a retail cooperative is usually returned to the consumers in the form of dividends based on the amounts purchased over a given period of time.

"Modern consumer cooperatives, usually called co-ops in the United States, are thought to have begun in Great Britain in 1844, with the Rochdale Society of Equitable Pioneers. The society created a set of organizational and working rules that have been widely adopted. They included open membership, democratic control, no religious or political discrimination, sales at prevailing market prices, and the setting aside of some earnings for education.

"The cooperative movement developed rapidly in the latter part of the 19th century. . . . It spread quickly among the urban working class in Britain, France, Germany, and Sweden and among the rural population of Norway, The Netherlands, Denmark, and Finland."

—*The New Encyclopedia Brittanica*, 1992, 15th Edition, Volume 3, p. 605

Folk High School

"... type of residential school for adults that is standard in Scandinavian countries and has also been adopted elsewhere in Europe. The concept of the folk high school was originated in Denmark by the theologian N. F. S. Grundtvig as a means of providing the common people with a knowledge of their history, religion, and cultural heritage.

"After Denmark's military defeat by Austria and Prussia in 1864, in which Slesvig, Holstein, and Laurenberg were lost until after World War II, these schools were a powerful instrument of national regeneration. There are no entrance qualifications or leaving examinations; attendance is completely voluntary. The atmosphere is homelike. Students and teachers live, work, and play together. The singing of hymns and folksongs is characteristic. Subjects of general interest in literature and social science predominate. Most students are young adults, originally rural workers, but now urban as well. The schools are private but receive state subsidies, and many attract an international body of students."

—*The New Encyclopedia Brittanica*, 1992, 15th Edition, Volume 4, p. 862.

International People's College

The International People's College was founded to apply Pastor N. F. S. Grundtvig's folk school concept to the international scene and at the college level. It drew staff and students from many countries. It was headed by Peter Manniche, whose wife, Emmy Louisa, was my double second cousin. She looked so much like me that people often confused us.

Treaty of Trianon

"Treaty concluding World War I and signed by representatives of Hungary on one side and the Allied Powers on the other. It was signed on June 4, 1920, at the Trianon Palace at Versailles, France.

"By the terms of the treaty, Hungary was shorn of at least two-thirds of its former territory and two-thirds of its inhabitants. Czechoslovakia was given Slovakia, sub-Carpathian Ruthenia, the region of Pressburg (Bratislava), and other minor sites. Austria received western Hungary (most of Burgenland). The Kingdom of Serbs, Croats, and Slovenes (Yugoslavia) took Croatia-Slavonia and part of the Banat. Romania received most of the Banat and all of Transylvania. Italy received Fiume. Except for plebiscites in two small regions, all the transfers were effected without any plebiscites.

"The Covenant of the League of Nations was integrally included in the treaty. Hungary's armed forces were to be restricted to 35,000 men, lightly armed and employed only to maintain internal order and to secure the frontiers. The amount of reparations to be imposed was to be determined later."

—*The New Encyclopedia Brittanica*, 1992, 15th Edition, Volume 11, p. 917

About the Author

Christine Morgan died on May 3, 1996. She had a long career in social activism and civil rights, served as Dean of Women at Rollins College in Winter Park, Florida, and organized the Human Relations Commission in Appleton, Wisconsin.